Cooking

Waylon's Way

Entertaining at Southern Comfort

Jessi Colter / Maureen Raffety

Cooking Waylon's Way
Copyright 2008 Jessi Colter and Maureen Raffety

Design and Archival by Warren Main Design
www.warrenmain.com

Ornaments by Nadine Pau - Saint Petersburg, Russia
www.nadinepau.blogspot.com
www.nadinepau.deviantart.com

Contents

Foreword

*I*n studies of students, researchers are finding a correlation between excelling in school and life and eating meals together as a family. The family meal remains a time of coming together that completes the day.

Introduction

Waylon was born in West Texas, I was born in Arizona, and Maureen Raffety, our "chief of staff," hails from Kentucky. Between the three of us, we have come up with meals that incorporate the taste of the West and the flair of the South.

Our menus were created by Maureen, while Waylon and I helped guide the delicate balance of unforgettable flavors. This is how the three of us spent much of our time.

Waylon had a voracious appetite and enjoyed a bountiful table three times a day. This inspired Maureen, whose culinary skills have thrilled guests that have joined us from all over the world.

We invite you into Southern Comfort, our Nashville, Tennessee home, where we have loved and laughed our way through life's ups and downs. We want to share these times with you. Our hope is that you will enjoy the humor along with the recipes that we have developed while working our way from rich, creamy butter to light, virgin olive oil.

Maureen, an educator by profession when we began managing Southern Comfort, didn't cook at all. However, Waylon developed high cholesterol and my taste buds changed when I was pregnant with our son, Shooter. Suddenly, we had to rethink our diets. I was at a loss as to how to plan meals we both could eat, without sacrificing the beauty and richness of the food. Maureen rose to the occasion and designed meals for our new lifestyle.

We will stir up twenty-five years of memories, humor and the joy of celebrating our lives together. May you savor the love of life and food along with us.

Jessi Colter

Thanksgiving 1975 - Cinnamon Hill, Estate of Johnny Cash in Jamaica

Waylon's name means "land by the highway," and we've seen most of the highways in the country, while never missing a meal that I can remember. We met in Scottsdale, Arizona in 1966 while he was recording a song called "Norwegian Wood." We were both married to other mates so our meeting was strictly business; he was a progressive new country star–I was a songwriter and recording artist who found him to be a gentleman.

When our marriages were ending, we became traveling companions in 1968. He was 32 and I was a mere 25 when we began our courtship and we married in 1969. Although we settled occasionally, most of our time was spent in busses, planes, cars and hotel rooms. Our culinary habits were "eat when you can, what you can...quickly."

We clashed right off because Waylon was always hungry and I was tired of cooking. I never asked questions first, so I charged my way into this long-legged, West Texan's honky-tonk world and "stirred up the beans." I should have known then that it wasn't going to be easy... but, oh the bliss of self-confidence and youth.

Waylon both fascinated and frightened me. He was a man of mystery from the start. How could I confidently cook for him when one-dish meals, sauces and Arizona-style cooking was my expertise? My husband didn't like casseroles or sauces. Well, who says you need to eat the first year of marriage?

In time I figured it out. Waylon liked everything fried, cooked separately, and well-done. He ate only white sugar and white bread and he wanted lots of food...right then!

I set out to show Waylon that I was as innovative a cook as any other self-respecting bride. When Waylon invited our good friends over to our apartment to eat, I decided to do it up right. What would set him on his heels? I'd roast a rack of lamb and introduce him to artichokes and mint jelly. Big mistake!

Knowing what food a man doesn't like usually tells a story about his upbringing. There were several well-meant directions I received early in our marriage and some of them remained throughout our years together.

Waylon's Do's and Don'ts

1. Don't prepare water gravy. It reminds him of days past when there was no milk in his refrigerator and he only had water to prepare gravy.

2. Don't reheat food. It reminds him of his grandmother's ability to kill the taste of food by repeated reheating.

3. NEVER undercook meat. Rare meat reminded him of too many years on the road and away from home.

4. Forget the casseroles. They make him think the cook is using leftovers. And, he doesn't care for their consistency.

5. Never boil okra - it's too slimy.

6. No lamb. It reminds him of sheep in the field - a big no, no.

All these dos and don'ts made us discriminating and friends looked to him for a steer in the right direction when eating out. He had a knack for telling what was the best offer in the house. Perhaps it was that West Texas "luck of the draw."

Guacamole

6 ripe avocados, peeled
2 tomatoes, coarsely chopped
1 cup grated Monterey Jack cheese
½ small red onion, chopped
½ teaspoon salt

½ teaspoon coriander
1 teaspoon cumin
1 clove garlic, minced
Juice of 1 lime
3 tablespoons olive oil

Place the avocados, tomatoes, cheese, onion, salt, coriander, cumin, garlic, lime juice and olive oil in a food processor. Use the pulse setting to coarsely blend.

Makes 2 cups

Mama's Hot Sauce

Two 28-ounce cans tomatoes
Two 28-ounce cans
   crushed tomatoes
4 cups sugar
5 jalapeño peppers, chopped
4 to 5 green peppers, chopped

3 medium onions,
   chopped
1 pod garlic,
   finely chopped
2 cups apple cider
   vinegar

Combine the tomatoes, jalapeño peppers, green peppers, onions, garlic, sugar and vinegar in a saucepan. Bring to a boil and lower the heat to a slow boil, stirring every 10 to 15 minutes. Simmer for 4 to 5 hours and reduce to half to create thickness. Pour the sauce into hot sterilized jars and seal lightly until cool. Store at room temperature or refrigerate. Excellent with eggs, chicken, beef or fish.

Makes twelve to fourteen 8-ounce jars

Smelling the hot vinegar and seeing the steam rise off Mama's stove sounded the alarm to stay out of the way when I ran in from school. Making hot sauce was an all day, once-a-year event and it's the only canning I saw her do. My sister, Mary D. Korman, continues the tradition today.

Mexican Hot Sauce

16-ounce can tomatoes
1 medium onion, chopped
1 tablespoon vinegar
½ teaspoon salt

2 cloves garlic
1 tablespoon sugar
4-ounce can green chiles

Combine the tomatoes and onion in a blender container and process. Add the vinegar, salt, garlic, sugar and green chiles and process. Try on eggs, baked potatoes, taco salads, etc.

Kentucky Knockouts

2 tablespoons butter
12 eggs, well beaten

8-ounce box Velveeta
  cheese, cut into
  small pieces
Salt and pepper to taste

Melt the butter in a skillet. Add the eggs and cheese, stirring occasionally. Season with the salt and pepper.

Serves 4 to 6

Phoenix Scramblers

2 eggs
1 teaspoon water
1 tablespoon milk

Pepper to taste
2 teaspoons butter

Break the eggs into a bowl. Add the water, milk and pepper. Beat the eggs well with a whisk or fork until light and fluffy.

Melt the butter in a skillet over a medium heat. Pour in the egg mixture and allow the eggs to set slightly. Stir gently until the eggs are set but still soft.

Serves 1

The secret with eggs is in the beating.

Sausage Gravy

1 pound pork sausage
4 heaping tablespoons flour

3 to 4 cups milk
Salt and pepper to taste

Brown the sausage in a skillet. Mash the sausage with the tines of a fork or a potato masher and drain. Return the sausage to the skillet and stir in the flour, cooking for 2 to 3 minutes. Add the milk, a small amount at a time, stirring continually. When the gravy thickens and bubbles it is ready. Season with the salt and pepper. Serve immediately over hot biscuits.

Serves 6

* If the gravy looks too dry you have used to much flour; add a little butter. If it is too wet, add a little flour. Stir well.

If there is one food in the world that Waylon loved more than anything, it is most assuredly sausage gravy with biscuits. In the early days, this was his daily breakfast but in later years it was saved for weekends when he was home. As time passed, it became only for special occasions and always on Christmas morning because of health and dietary restrictions. Sausage gravy was also served at the East meets West breakfast for west coast and New York records executives. Unlike Southerners, the guests didn't care for the gravy. Some called it a cream sauce and most had never seen anything like it.

Many nights we gathered in the kitchen and watched as Mama mixed up the sugar and cocoa for the fudge. We loved licking the spoon as the fudge hardened.

Our desert cabin was near the Gila (pronounced Heela) River 90 miles southeast of Mesa, Arizona, as the crow flies. Just us, God, the coyotes, rattlers and scorpions reigned over that 1200 acre expanse. My engineering father had built the mills there and mined for copper ore and molybdenum for many years. He was a true mountain man, afraid of nothing. On the other hand Mama was always in the kitchen thanking God and singing hymns. These are warm places in my heart.

Mama's Fudge

3 cups sugar
⅔ cup cocoa
⅛ teaspoon salt
1½ cups milk

¼ cup (½ stick) butter
  or margarine
1 teaspoon vanilla
  extract

Combine the sugar, cocoa and salt in a heavy saucepan. Stir in the milk. Cook over a medium heat, stirring constantly, until the mixture comes to a full rolling boil. Boil, without stirring, to 234 degrees Fahrenheit on a candy thermometer or until it resembles syrup. The mixture should form a soft ball when dropped into very cold water. Add the butter and vanilla extract. Do not stir. Cool the fudge at room temperature until lukewarm. Beat the fudge with a wooden spoon until the fudge thickens and loses some of its gloss. Spread the fudge quickly into a buttered 9-inch baking dish; cool. Cut the fudge into squares.

Makes about 36 squares

Beef Stroganoff à la Jessi

1 ½ pounds sirloin,
  cut into narrow strips
½ onion, chopped
¼ cup butter or margarine
10¾-ounce can
  cream of chicken soup

¼ cup water
Sherry cooking wine
Fresh mushrooms, sliced
1 cup sour cream

Sauté the sirloin and onion in the butter until the red is gone from the meat. Add the soup and water. Bring the mixture to a slow simmer for 10 to 15 minutes. Add a dash or two of the sherry. Stir in the mushrooms and simmer for 5 minutes. Stir in the sour cream; bring to a simmer and remove from the heat. Add more wine before serving. Pour over wild rice.

Serves 4

Maureen's Beef Stroganoff

6 tablespoons all-purpose flour
½ teaspoon paprika
1½ teaspoons salt
¼ teaspoon pepper
2 pounds sirloin,
   cut into narrow strips
½ cup butter
4 small onions, chopped
2 cloves garlic

2 tablespoons
   tomato paste
½ teaspoon sugar
Two 14-ounce cans
   chicken broth
1½ cups fresh
   mushrooms, sliced
2 cups sour cream
¼ cup chopped parsley
Dash of paprika

Combine the flour, paprika, salt and pepper in a bowl. Dredge the meat in the flour mixture. Melt a small amount of the butter in a skillet. Add the sirloin strips and brown quickly on both sides. Remove the beef and drain on paper towels; set aside. Add the remaining butter and sauté the onions and garlic until the onions are tender. Add the tomato paste, sugar and meat; cover with the chicken broth. Cover and simmer gently for 1½ to 2 hours or until the meat is tender. Add the mushrooms and sour cream 30 minutes before serving and cook slowly. Add the parsley and paprika for color and simmer for 5 minutes. Serve over buttered noodles.

Serves 6 to 8

Mama's Meat Loaf

1 pound ground beef
¼ pound pork sausage
⅓ cup bread crumbs
⅓ cup milk
1 egg, beaten
2 tablespoons finely-chopped
    onion

½ teaspoon
    Seasoned salt
½ teaspoon salt
Dash of pepper
¼ cup ketchup
or chili sauce

Combine the ground beef, pork sausage, bread crumbs, milk, egg, onion, Accent seasoning, salt and pepper in a large bowl and mix well. Place the mixture in a loaf pan.

Bake at 350 degrees for 30 minutes. Glaze with the ketchup or chili sauce and bake for 15 minutes.

Remove the meat loaf to a warm platter and skim the fat from the sauce. Pour the sauce over the meat loaf.

Serves 5

Note: For individual servings, shape into 4 to 5 small loaves and bake in a 9x13-inch baking dish.

Mama's Roast

4 to 5 pound shoulder roast
Garlic salt
Garlic powder
Onion salt
Pepper
Lemon pepper
1 cup flour

½ cup canola oil
2 onions, quartered
8 carrots,
    cut into 2-inch chunks
3 stalks celery
1 jalapeño pepper
4 to 5 potatoes,
    quartered

Season the roast generously with the garlic salt, garlic powder, onion salt, pepper, and lemon pepper. Dredge the roast in the flour.

Heat the oil in a skillet or Dutch oven to a boil. Sear the roast on both sides until the flour and seasonings form a golden crust.

Place the roast in a roasting pan or Dutch oven and cover half way with water. Add the onions. Bake at 350 degrees for 3 to 4 hours or until tender. Add the carrots, celery, jalapeño and potatoes the last hour of cooking. Cook until the vegetables are tender.

Prime Rib Roast

6-7 pound standing prime rib roast
Freshly ground pepper
Garlic Powder

Salt, coarsly ground, such as sea salt
Fresh finely chopped Parsley

Select a roast that will allow at least 1/2 pound per person, or 2 people per rib. Generously rub the roast with alive oil, salt, garlic, parsley, and lots of freshly ground pepper. Stand the roast, fat side up in a baking pan with a rack. Place in a pre-heated 500 degree oven for 15 minutes.

Turn the heat down to 325 degrees and continue roasting, allowing 13-15 minutes per pound for rare and 15-17 for medium rare. Check with a meat thermometer. A reading of 120-125 degrees will be rare, 130-135 degrees for medium rare, 135-140 for medium, and 150-155 for medium well.

Popovers

2 eggs
1 cup milk

1 cup sifted all-purpose
   flour
¼ teaspoon salt

Place the eggs and milk in a blender container. Cover and process on high speed until frothy. Stop and add the flour and salt. Process again until smooth. Pour the batter into coated muffin pans or custard cups. Bake at 450 degrees for 20 minutes. Reduce the heat to 350 degrees and bake for 10 to 15 minutes.

Makes 8 to 10 popovers

Chicken Marsala

2 ounces butter
2 boneless, skinless chicken breasts
½ cup flour
Paprika
Pinch of salt
Pinch of pepper
1 teaspoon crushed garlic

½ medium onion, chopped
1½ ounces fresh mushrooms, sliced
Juice of ½ lemon
¾ ounces marsala wine

Heat the butter in a skillet. Dust the chicken with the flour and sprinkle with the paprika. Brown the chicken in the skillet. Sprinkle the chicken with the salt, pepper and garlic. Cook the chicken thoroughly. Add the onion, mushrooms, capers and lemon juice. Add the marsala wine and cook 10 minutes.

Serves 2

Waylon's Chicken-Fried Chicken and Gravy

One of Waylon's favorite dishes was chicken-fried steak. He came up with this recipe as a way to replace red meat.

2 cups flour
1 teaspoon garlic powder
½ teaspoon pepper
½ teaspoon paprika
½ cup cream
2 eggs, beaten

8 thin boneless
   breast fillets
Melted shortening
   or butter
¼ cup flour
2 to 3 cups milk
Salt and pepper to taste

Season the flour with the garlic powder, pepper and paprika in a bowl. Combine the eggs and cream in a separate bowl and beat well. Dredge the chicken in the seasoned flour, dip the chicken into the egg mixture, and dredge again in the flour.

Place the chicken in a heavy skillet with ½ inch of the melted shortening. Cook for 3 to 5 minutes per side or until golden brown. The chicken cooks quickly because it is very thin. Remove the chicken from the skillet and drain all but 2 to 3 tablespoons of the grease, to make the gravy. Put 3 tablespoons of the flour in the grease and stir until the mixture foams. Slowly add the milk. Turn the heat down and continue to cook for 3 minutes when the gravy begins to thicken. Season with the salt and pepper. Serve immediately over the chicken-fried chicken. Mashed potatoes or rice, a salad and hot biscuits make this a fine southern dinner.

Note: I use half butter and half canola oil. The butter gives it a wonderful flavor, but you need the oil because you can't heat butter as hot as needed for frying.

Mama's Goulash

1 tablespoon cooking oil
1½ pounds ground round
½ cup chopped onion
¼ cup chopped green pepper
½ teaspoon garlic salt
1 teaspoon chili powder

2 tablespoons
  picante sauce
Two 8-ounce cans
  tomato sauce
1 tablespoon sugar
8-ounce box bite-size
  elbow macaroni

This is a recipe that Waylon remembered his mother preparing for the family when he was a child. He loved it as a child and fondly remembered it as an adult.

Heat the oil in a large skillet and brown the ground round well. Add the onion, pepper, garlic salt, chili powder and picante sauce. Sauté until the onion is tender. Add the tomato sauce and sugar; simmer for 20 minutes.

Cook the macaroni according to the package directions; drain and stir the macaroni into the meat mixture. Add a little water or tomato sauce if the goulash is too dry. Simmer for 5 to 10 minutes. Serve immediately. This along with a salad and good bread is all you need for a fast, filling and tasty supper.

New England Clam Chowder

¼ pound bacon, diced
2 cups finely-chopped onion
3 cups diced potatoes
½ teaspoon dried thyme
2 cups chicken broth

4 cups finely-chopped
   canned clams
   with their liquid
4 cups milk
2 tablespoons butter
Salt and pepper to taste

Cook the bacon in a stockpot until crisp. Add the onion and cook until the onion is transparent, stirring constantly. Add the potatoes, thyme and broth and cook for 12 minutes or until the potatoes are tender. Add the clams, milk, butter, salt and pepper and cook for 10 minutes.

Serves 10

Waylon's Corn Chowder

½ pound bacon
1 large onion, diced
1 cup diced celery
½ cup all-purpose flour
2 quarts chicken stock
2 cups peeled, diced potatoes
½ teaspoon thyme
1 bay leaf

4 sprigs parsley
6 peppercorns, crushed
1 clove garlic
6 ears (2 cups)
   sweet corn
2 tablespoons butter
2 cups half-and-half
Salt and pepper to taste

Sauté the bacon in a 4-quart stockpot until the bacon is crisp. Remove the bacon with a slotted spoon and discard it, leaving the fat in the stockpot. Add the onion and celery and sauté until the onion is transparent. Add the flour and cook over a low heat for 10 minutes, without browning. Add the chicken stock and bring the mixture to a boil, stirring until no lumps remain. Reduce the heat to a simmer and add the potatoes, thyme, bay leaf, parsley, peppercorns and garlic.

Cut the corn off the cob with a sharp knife, being careful not to cut the cob. Add the corn to the soup. Continue simmering until the potatoes are tender. Add the butter and half-and-half. Season with the salt and pepper. Ladle the chowder into bowls and garnish with parsley.

Serves 8 to 10

Lorene's Pea Salad

Carrots, shredded
Green pepper, diced
Green peas, drained
Green onions, chopped

Shredded Cheddar
or American cheese
2 teaspoons mayonnaise

Combine the carrots, green pepper, peas, onions, cheese and mayonnaise in a bowl and mix well. Refrigerate until ready to serve.

The amounts will be determined by taste. We like to go light on the carrots and cheese. A fast-moving favorite.

The Traveling Years

Jessi in award winning Mac Truck named "Miss Jessi"

The excitement of new places never dies. However, something happens when the earth beneath you moves. I've searched high and low to find ways to deal with the problem of jet-lag, bus-lag and the physical and emotional drain of traveling. I can look at another entertainer and guess how long he's been on the road. The road is a place in time and no place at all.

The only advice I can give is learn to pace yourself; eat right and rest well. Prepare meals in your confined space that will satisfy both your needs and wants.

Cooking on the Bus

"We'll roll at midnight," is a familiar call of road life. And "Be prepared," is absolutely a necessary motto.

Before we left, our bus was always stocked by our driver. In the old days we ate "Whataburgers," milkshakes barbecued ribs, French fries and bologna sandwiches. We made sausage gravy with biscuits, taco salads, beans and corn bread, omelets and Mexican-style tortilla eggs. And, we always had a pot of coffee on the fire.

Calling Ahead

In the late seventies Dr. Constantine Potannin, a cardiologist and the director of the Cardiovascular Department at Baptist Hospital in Nashville, Tennessee, examined Waylon. In his own charming Australian way, he winced as he pronounced Waylon's blood "as thick as honey." That statement was enough to make Waylon think differently about food. Stressing that Waylon's future food choices would determine his life-span, the young doctor got Waylon's attention.

Maureen's ability to work under pressure was put to the test when she became our culinary guide. She innovated recipes from the list of acceptable foods which the doctor gave Waylon. She also designed recipes that could be reproduced by hotel chefs across the nation so that we could order meals ahead of time to keep Waylon eating right. From eighteen eggs a week to a seven-grain cereal with skim milk was a big

change, but within *six months*, Dr. Potannin found that Waylon's cholesterol had dropped to a healthy level.

High Energy Foods

I've always believed that entertainers should eat like athletes. Although there's not the same rigid physical discipline, life on the road is demanding. I'm told athletes eat a diet of 20% protein, 60% complex carbohydrates, and 20% fat.

While many people would rather have small portions of many kinds of foods, Waylon was interested in big portions. So, for a 20/60/20 combination, rather than have 3,000 calories with 600 protein/1,800 complex carbohydrates/600 fat calories, he would choose large amounts of food at one sitting but would not exercise enough to burn 3,000 calories. He wanted to be healthy and loose weight; so to achieve this he lowered his food intake to 2,000 calories and exercised 30 minutes, three times a week. After I finish these higher mathematics, I'll tell you what that means!

Jennings

Side A
You Never Can Tell (C'est La Vie) (3:12)
Rainy Seasons (2:34)
I'll Be Alright (1:53)
Wild Side of Life (3:20)
Pastels and Harmony (3:18)

Side B
I Believe You Can (2:56)
What's Happened to Blue Eyes (2:32)
Storms Never Last (3:08)
I Ain't the One (2:25)
You're Not My Same Sweet Baby (3:47)

right, Jerry Bridges,
e Mooney, Bucky
Buttrey, Norbert

idges, Carter Robertson.

, Paradise Valley, Arizona.

ion: Herb Burnette.

June Carter Cash's Vegetable Stuff

Delicious with steak or barbecued chicken or as a light meal. Feel free to experiment and add your favorite vegetables to create your own version of "stuff."

1 pound fresh mushrooms
1 large green pepper,
    sliced ¼-inch thick
½ cup oil
2 medium green tomatoes,
    sliced
2 zucchini,
    sliced ¼-inch thick
½ cup flour

⅛ teaspoon
    freshly-ground pepper
½ teaspoon salt
1 pound potatoes,
    peeled and thinly sliced
1 cup chopped onion
½ teaspoon salt
¼ cup butter
    or margarine
1 teaspoon sugar

Rinse the mushrooms, pat dry and slice. Sauté the green pepper in ¼ cup of the oil in a large skillet for 2 minutes; remove the pepper with a slotted spoon. Dredge the tomatoes and zucchini in a mixture of the flour, pepper and salt. Sauté 2 to 3 slices at a time for 2 minutes on each side or until brown; remove the vegetables with a slotted spoon. Heat the remaining ¼ cup oil in the skillet. Add the potatoes, onion and salt. Cook until the potatoes are tender, stirring frequently. Remove the vegetables with a slotted spoon. Sauté the mushrooms in the butter for 5 minutes. Stir in the sugar, additional salt and pepper. Add the sautéed vegetables; tossing gently. Heat to serving temperature and serve immediately. Toss with freshly grated Parmesan cheese if desired.

Serves 4

Maureen's Vegetable Lasagna

1 medium onion, chopped
2 cloves of garlic
1 tablespoon olive oil
8 ounces sliced mushrooms
1/2 pound fresh baby spinach
1 teaspoon freshly ground pepper
2 eggs
Salt to taste

4 teaspoons of sugar
16 ounce carton ricotta cheese
4 cups of shredded mozzarella cheese
1/2 cup parmesan cheese
12 ounces fresh mozzarella
32 ounces spaghetti sauce
9 lasagna noodles
1 bunch parsley

Sauté the onion in olive oil until translucent, add the garlic, the mushrooms and the spinich. To this add the spaghetti sauce, salt, sugar, and fresh ground pepper.

In a bowl combine ricotta, 1 cup of shredded mozzarella, 1/2 cup of parmesan cheese, eggs, salt, and freshly ground pepper.

Cook the noodles to the al dente stage. Drain the noodles on paper towel to absorb any excess water.

Coat the bottom of a 9x13 baking dish with a small amount of olive oil. Lay 3 of the noodles on the bottom of the dish, top with 8 ounces of fresh mozzarella cheese. Sprinkle with salt, pepper, and fresh, finely chopped parsley, next place 1/2 of the vegatable and sauce mixture, then 1/2 of the egg and cheese mixture. Repeat with 3 more noodles, salt, fresh pepper, and parsley, another layer of fresh mozzarella, the rest of the sauce, and the rest of the cheese and egg mixture. Top with the remaining noodles, **salt, freshly ground pepper**, and chopped parsley. Sprinkle with 3 cups of shredded mozzarella cheese.

Bake at 350 degrees for 45 minutes covered, uncover and bake 15 minutes longer, or until the cheese on top is melted and slighty brown. Allow the lasagna to cool 10-15 minutes before slicing.

Note: for meat lovers, add chopped meat to the sauce, such as beef.

Spaghetti and Meatballs

You can make the meatballs any size you like. If they are small, you will yield approximately 30. We like ours larger, therefor, we get only about 18.

1 large onion, chopped
3 cloves garlic
3 tablespoons olive oil
Two 6-ounce cans
　　tomato paste
29-ounce can tomato sauce
10¾-ounce can tomato purée
1 teaspoon garlic salt
2 tablespoons sugar
1 teaspoon salt
1 tablespoon sweet basil
1 bay leaf
¼ teaspoon pepper
1 teaspoon pepper

¾ cup milk
¾ pound ground veal
¾ pound ground sirloin
½ cup chopped onion
2 eggs
½ cup grated
　　Parmesan cheese
1 teaspoon garlic salt
½ teaspoon dried
　　oregano
2 tablespoons finely-
　　chopped fresh parsley
3 tablespoons canola oil
6 slices of bread
2 pounds spaghetti

　　Sauté the onion and garlic in the olive oil until the onion is tender. Stir in the tomato paste, tomato sauce, tomato purée, 1 teaspoon garlic salt, sugar, salt, basil, bay leaf and the 1 teaspoon of pepper. Simmer uncovered for several hours, until thick and flavorful.

　　Soak the bread in the milk until the bread has soaked up all the liquid. Combine the veal, sirloin, onion, eggs, cheese, 1 teaspoon garlic salt, oregano, parsley and the ¼ teaspoon of pepper in a large bowl. Add the bread, combining thoroughly.

　　Form the mixture into balls using wet hands. Brown the meatballs slowly in the canola oil; drain. Add the meatballs to the sauce, simmer and loosely cover the last 30 minutes of cooking.

　　Prepare the spaghetti according to the package directions.

Serves 6 to 8

Cream of Tomato Soup

3 cloves garlic, minced
4 cups finely-chopped onion
½ cup oil
¼ cup butter
2 cups celery tops,
   finely chopped
16 cups tomato purée
1 tablespoon sugar

3 tablespoons salt
2 cups water
2 cups chicken broth
8 bay leaves
3 whole black
   peppercorns
2 cups heavy cream
Three 10¾-ounce cans
   condensed tomato
   soup

Sauté the garlic and onion in the oil and butter in a heavy saucepan. Add the celery, tomato purée, sugar, salt, water, broth, bay leaves and peppercorns. Bring the mixture to a boil; reduce the heat and simmer uncovered for 1 hour. Press the mixture through a coarse sieve or process until smooth in a blender container. Stir in the cream and tomato soup and heat.

Serves 20

Waylon, Shooter and Jessi at Southern Comfort

The Family Years

Ten years of marriage brought us to mid-life. Only through God's grace did we live to tell the story. Failure and success tested us but we felt a surge of new confidence. We committed to a new beginning with the birth of our son, Shooter.

In this section, we share recipes for dishes served at Shooter's christening, with our special guests Muhammad Ali and Johnny Cash; Waylon's birthday party, with idols of his youth; Shooter's sixth birthday, with the super heroes of the day, He-Man and Skeletor; and the unveiling of Storms Never Last, bust of Waylon.

A Night To Remember:
Christening Shooter

Our son, Waylon Albright Jennings "Shooter," is the most beautiful gift we've ever had. We celebrated with his christening on July 25, 1979.

Several days before, a white tent was set up and the summer breeze seemed charged with excitement. Our backyard began to bloom with white caladiums, white mums and white impatiens laced with tender ferns, all planted just for the celebration. Under the tent, tables and white garden chairs awaited more than two hundred guests.

The invitation read:

If You've Ever Been In Love
We would like to invite you to share in our joy
as magnolias, moonlight, and a candlelight dinner
set the stage for the christening of

Waylon Albright Jennings

on Wednesday, the Twenty-fifth of July
Eight O'clock at our home.
Bring love, thanksgiving, and be ready for
a night to remember.

Waylon & Jessi

After a week of preparation, we were greeted at dawn with a torrential downpour that was to continue all day. The caterer and florist struggled to work their magic against all odds.

After twelve hours of nonstop rain, the clock struck 8:00 p.m. The guests arrived. The rain

Waylon Albright Jennings AKA Shooter

stopped. It was a miracle.

Our guests were people we worked with, our family and friends. They were diverse and included representatives from all walks of life. Some of the people who had traveled long distances to be there were Neil Reshen, of New York; Jay Goldberg, the famed New York criminal lawyer and his wife, Rema; Bob Sikora, of Bobby McGee's restaurants; William Hamilton, the decorator; Eloise Jeffries, the Southeast's first lady of Primitive American Antiques; Roupen Gulbenk, who sells museum quality antiques; and Frances Preston of Broadcast Music Inc. (BMI). Muhammad Ali, our hero, thrilled us by accepting our invitation to attend. And last, but not least, our good friend, Johnny Cash, who would later become Shooter's adopted godfather, was in attendance. Our favorite ministers–Will Campbell and Reverend Harris-and his wife, Mary, graced the scene and added blessings. There were representatives from the media and politics. John Jay Hooker, the last of a dying breed of the wonderful old southern politicians was with us. My obstetrician, Dr. Larry Arnold, attended and the list goes on and on. A remarkable variety of people came together in a most unforgettable way as a string quartet gently played classical music.

We offered the guests tasty hors d'oeuvres: bowls piled high with tantalizing shrimp, exotic fruits, and trays filled with puff pastries stuffed with mushrooms. Sparkling white wine generously flowed as we mingled.

Reverend Will Campbell was calmer than I as we prepared for the christening. We didn't want Shooter to tire, so we arranged for the ceremony to be early in the evening. He was already excited by all the activity and puzzled by the many guests peeking at him in his 1800s teester crib, a gift from Mary Sue and Roupen Gulbenk.

During the ceremony, I held Shooter in my arms, with Waylon standing on my right. Reverend Campbell stood between Waylon and Shooter's godparents, Maureen Raffety and Neil Reshen. Will began a most beautiful and original ceremony in which he thanked God for Shooter's safe arrival into this world and for my well-being during delivery. He declared Waylon Albright Jennings a manchild of the Lord and asked for God's blessing on our home. It was a reverent and holy event, led by a man of God and a true artist with a great command of the English language. I could not have been more touched by Will's heartfelt blessing.

As the ceremony proceeded, however, Shooter began to cry. I tried every little trick in the book to quiet him: first his pacifier, next the over-the-shoulder position, then the "pat on the bottom" routine. With all eyes on me, I began to break out in a sweat and my heart began to beat faster and faster. What could I do? As usual, Waylon stepped in with perfect timing and whispered, "Give him to me." I panicked because it had never been Waylon's practice to calm the baby. I once caught him bending over the cradle (the gold one Willie and Connie Nelson gave us) trying to make Shooter laugh after I'd spent hours getting him ready to go to sleep. But Waylon prided himself on his ability to get a reaction from Shooter and had told Frances Preston that night that he could get Shooter to do anything he wanted! Well, don't you know it, Shooter hushed up when his Daddy took him

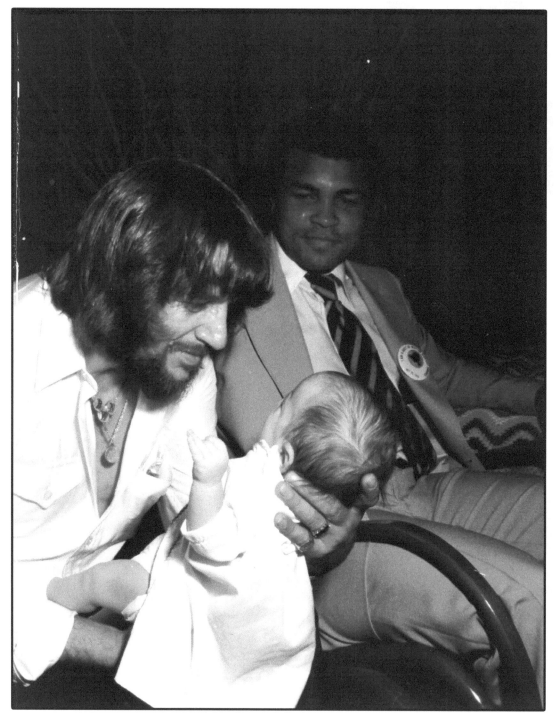

Shooter's Christening, July 25, 1979 - Waylon, Shooter and Muhammed Ali

and Will was able to finish the ceremony. I couldn't believe it. The mother works endlessly to soothe and care for the baby and the daddy gets the credit!

Soon it was time for Shooter to return to his domain and for the party to continue on the hill.

As our friends made their way outside, they passed magnolias and candles floating on the pool which lit the way to the festive dinner. I remember taking Muhammad Ali's arm and walking him out to the tennis court where the big tent stood. I'll never forget the balance he had and the way his strong body moved from side to side as he walked. He was full of jokes that night. He carried a little buzzer that he used to shock the ladies when he went up behind them. Then he'd stand back and look all innocent when they turned around in dismay. When he met a couple he'd ask the woman if that's the best she could do.

We served baked tenderloin with béarnaise and remoulade sauces. We had asparagus and fresh corn soufflé, because both vegetables were in season. We ate lobster tails, a beautiful summer vegetable salad and lots of homemade breads. Our dessert buffet offered Waldorf Astoria cake, beautiful tarts, pastries filled with rich cream and oversized strawberries with luscious hot fudge for dipping. French coffee, served with whipped cream and chocolate sprinkles, topped off an evening filled with warmth, meaning and good food.

Waylon's Forty-Fourth Birthday Party

Waylon's forty-fourth birthday, June 15th, called for a royal celebration. We decided to gather together many of his present friends who had been his idol, or role model, during his youth. We thought this was a perfect way to celebrate such an important turning point in Waylon's life.

Our preparations began and we hired an events coordinator, An Affair to Remember. They created a country western theme on our tennis court for the big night. A large white tent was set up, tables were brought in and a stage was erected. We thought we had it planned perfectly, since Waylon was out of town doing a show the night before and would not return until 7:00 p.m., and the party started at 8:00 p.m. True to Waylon's nature, however, he walked in the house at 4:00 that afternoon and said, "Where's my party?" In the background the caterers were running around, the tent was in full view, the parking valets were out front and the press had arrived. Of course, we replied, "What party?"

So, the ruse was up and the party began. Red O'Donnell, a columnist for *The Tennessean* wanted a family photo of Waylon, Shooter and me. During the photo session our two-year old, Shooter, didn't want to smile. With much encouragement he finally gave his famous "movie star" smile. The picture appeared in the morning paper the next day and from then on Shooter was famous for his smile.

Our guest list included Carl Smith and his beautiful and talented wife, Goldie Hill; Jimmy Dickens, and the lovely Mona Dickens; Hank Williams, Jr.; Tony Joe and LeAnn White; Chet Atkins and Ernest Tubb and his Texas Troubadours. Many of the Nashville, New York and Los Angeles record executives were also there.

Jim Neal, Watergate, attorney; many government officials; Will Campbell, author and minister; Jamie Carter of Jamie Inc.; and many friends, including Bob Sikora of Arizona were also present. The night was sprinkled with Nashville's finest stars.

Delicious western barbecue that included brisket, ribs and chicken was served. We had summer vegetables, salads, breads and the largest cake you can imagine. It was topped with 44 brightly burning candles and it took four people to roll it out.

The dress was western attire, and of course, Little Jimmy Dickens was the most colorful. He wore an orange suit complete with hat and rhinestones! I was in a dazzling purple outfit and Shooter was dressed as a miniature Waylon.

The music was bluegrass and was provided by the Billy and Terry Smith group. There were also many songs performed by the guests that highlighted the event.

Hank Williams, Jr. came bearing a fine antique firearm as a gift and Carl Smith jokingly offered his wife, Goldie, as a prize!

The night was a memorable celebration and one of our most successful events at Southern Comfort.

Shooter's Sixth Birthday

It was a special day in May for a truly special boy as we celebrated Shooter's sixth birthday. The party consisted of an array of festivities that were nothing short of spectacular. The theme was an amusement park featuring Super Heroes!

There were several game booths to test

He-Man and Skeletor surprise Shooter.

their skills. Each booth was full of prizes, so each child would leave a winner. The menu was hot dogs, hamburgers, French fries and apple pie: this was truly an all-American party complete with cotton candy. Clowns acted as waiters and also provided entertainment. There were helium-filled balloons, jugglers, acrobats and clowns on unicycles. A giant-sized moon walk and an arena for toy turtle rides added to the fun.

The festivities included Mattel's sensational hit of the eighties, Masters of the Universe, featuring the phenomenal He-Man and his nemesis, Skeletor. What else could the cake be but a Castle Grayskull featuring the characters from Masters of the Universe?

The swimming pool had a rainbow arch of balloons across it. Masters of the Universe helium balloons were attached to each garden chair. There were all types of party favors and toys including horns, streamers and swords, so that each child could be like He-Man.

The most memorable surprise was the live appearance of Mattel's own He-Man and Skeletor. The characters were in town on a promotional tour. Waylon had made a few well-placed phone calls and they agreed to come, which was unheard of as they ordinarily never came to private parties. They gave out autographs, posters, handshakes and participated in numerous sword fights. The children either stared in awe, sat in the laps of the Masters or were tossed upon their shoulders. All of the children were thrilled.

As the party came to a close, clowns gave the children rides on unicycles and every balloon was given away. The fifty guests left with their arms full of prizes and some very special memories.

Unveiling of "Storms Never Last"

Some years back I had a reception for John Hampton, founder of the Cowboy Artists of America and the originator of the Red Ryder cartoon. Through my sister, Sharon, I met Jim Branscum, an upcoming artist in the West. He'd done a beautiful book depicting the Indians of Arizona in their traditional dress and local setting. His work reminded me of the early American artists on the plains who first brought the knowledge of the Indian's art to the East.

We became friends and after seeing his work in sculpture, I commissioned him to do a bust of Waylon for me. Perhaps the art would not be in our home today had he not become ill with pancreatitis. But Jim thrived on a challenge. Though he became ill and grew weak, he asked if he could begin the bust of Waylon. I said yes. Looking back, I feel perhaps it gave him the will to live, which he needed at that time.

Woody Crumbo's daughter, Minisa Halsey, helped me organize the unveiling party. Again, Will Campbell joined us and asked a blessing upon our home that night. Afterward, the Heard Museum in Scottsdale, Arizona put the bust on display.

Bust of Waylon entitled "Storms Never Last" by Sculptor Jim Branscum

Lorianne Crook, Will D. Campbell
Jessi, Waylon and Jim Branscum

left: **Our dear friends former Kentucky Governor and First Lady, Wallace and Martha Wilkerson.**

Princess Butter Corn Bread

2 eggs
1½ cups buttermilk
1½ cups cornmeal
½ cup flour
¼ to ½ cup sugar

3 teaspoons
  baking powder
¼ teaspoon soda
1 teaspoon salt
½ cup shortening
  or 1 stick butter

Beat the eggs and add the buttermilk. Sift the cornmeal, flour, sugar, baking power, soda and salt in a separate bowl. Add the dry mixture to the egg mixture. The batter will be thin to make a light, tender bread. Heat the shortening in an iron skillet or square baking dish. Pour the hot shortening into the batter and mix well. Pour the batter into the skillet or dish. Bake at 450 degrees for 20 to 25 minutes.

Southwest Corn Bread

Bacon drippings
1½ cups self-rising cornmeal
1¼ cups buttermilk
1 tablespoon sugar
1 cup grated sharp cheese
½ cup vegetable oil
1 medium onion, chopped

1 teaspoon crushed
  red pepper or
1 teaspoon
  jalapeño pepper
2 eggs
One 8½-ounce can
  cream-style corn

Heat the bacon drippings in an iron skillet or corn stick pans. Combine the cornmeal, buttermilk, sugar, cheese, vegetable oil, onion, pepper, eggs and corn. Mix well and pour the batter into the hot skillet or pans. Bake for 30 minutes or until brown.

Serves 6 to 8

Cheese Grits

1 cup grits
3½ cups water
1 teaspoon salt
1 stick butter

8 ounces
   Velveeta cheese, cubed
2 eggs
½ cup milk

Cook the grits in the water with the salt added. Add the butter and cheese. Break the eggs in a measuring cup and add the milk. Mix well and add the egg mixture to the grits. Pour the mixture into a buttered casserole dish and bake at 350 degrees for 30 to 35 minutes or until set.

Chocolate Meringue Pie

This was Waylon's favorite.

4 eggs, separated
1 cup milk
1 cup half-and-half
1½ cups sugar
½ cup cocoa
2 teaspoon cornstarch
¼ teaspoon salt

3 tablespoons butter
2 teaspoons
  vanilla extract
¼ teaspoon
  cream of tartar
¼ teaspoon salt
3 tablespoons sugar

Beat the egg yolks. Add the milk and half-and-half. Combine the 1½ cups sugar, cocoa, cornstarch and salt in the top of a double boiler. Add the egg mixture and mix well. Cook this over hot, not boiling water, stirring constantly until thickened. Add the butter and vanilla extract and mix well. Remove the double boiler from the heat and allow the mixture to cool. Pour the mixture into a baked piecrust.

Beat the egg whites with the cream of tartar and the salt until stiff. Add 3 tablespoons of sugar, sprinkling over the egg whites and continue beating until the egg whites look like whipped cream. Spread the meringue over the chocolate pie and bake at 350 degrees until the meringue is brown.

Johnny Cash, George Richie and Tammy Wynette.

Fudge Cake Brownies

½ cup butter, melted
    (no substitute)
1 cup sugar
2 eggs, separated

2 ounces unsweetened
    chocolate, melted
1 teaspoon vanilla
    extract
1 cup chopped pecans
½ cup all-purpose flour

Cream the butter and sugar. Add the egg yolks and beat until light and fluffy. Blend in the chocolate and vanilla extract. Beat the egg whites until they are stiff. Fold the egg whites into the chocolate mixture. Toss the pecans in the flour and add the pecans to the chocolate mixture. Pour the mixture into a coated 8-or 9-inch square pan and bake for 20 minutes.

Makes 9 squares

Party for the unveiling of "Storms Never Last"

Peach Cobbler

4 cups peeled and
  sliced peaches
½ cup water
1½ cups sugar
2 tablespoons flour
¼ teaspoon salt
¾ cup butter, melted
2 cups flour

1 tablespoon
  baking powder
½ teaspoon salt
¼ teaspoon soda
¾ cup shortening
4 tablespoons
  cold water or milk
1½ teaspoons sugar

Cook the peaches in the ½ cup of water in a saucepan until the peaches are tender. Whisk in the 1½ cups sugar, the 2 tablespoons of flour and ¼ teaspoon salt and blend until smooth. Stir in the butter and mix well.

Blend the 2 cups of flour, baking powder, ½ teaspoon salt, soda and shortening until it is a coarse meal texture. Add the water or milk. Roll the dough on a floured pastry board. Pour the peaches into a 9x13-inch baking dish. Top with the dough. Sprinkle the 1½ teaspoons of sugar on top of the crust and dot with butter. Bake at 400 degrees for 30 minutes. Lower the heat to 350 degrees and bake for 30 minutes or until golden brown.

Waylon, Jessi, Buddy, Terry, Debra, and Jennifer Jennings.

Waylon's Favorite Apple Dumplings

2 cups water
½ teaspoon cinnamon
2 cups sugar
½ cup butter
2 cups all-purpose flour
1 teaspoon salt

⅔ cup shortening
4 tablespoons water
6 apples,
  peeled and sliced
2 tablespoons butter,
  cold

Combine the 2 cups of water, cinnamon and sugar in a saucepan. Bring the mixture to a boil and reduce the heat. Simmer the mixture for 15 to 20 minutes and add the ½ cup of butter. Set the mixture aside.

Combine the flour and salt. Cut half of the shortening into the flour mixture with a pastry blender or fork until it resembles cornmeal. Cut the remaining shortening in until it forms shapes the size of peas. Sprinkle the dough with the 4 tablespoons of water. Blend the water into the dough. Add an additional 1 teaspoon to 1 tablespoon of water if it is too dry. Gather the dough into a ball and divide into six portions. Roll each portion into a thin 6 to 8-inch circle.

Place ½ cup of the apples in the center of each circle. Sprinkle the apples with sugar and a touch of cinnamon; dot the apples with the cold butter. Fold the dough around the apples until you have a neat package. Repeat until all six are finished.

Place the dumplings in a 9x13-inch baking dish. Pour the sauce mixture over the apples. Bake at 375 degrees for 45 minutes to 1 hour or until the dumplings are brown and crusty on top. Serve warm with ice cream or pure cream over the top (about 2 tablespoons per dumpling).

Serves 6

Cousin Paul and Aunt Pearl's Spaghetti Sauce

Waylon loved this recipe and often requested it.

2 pounds ground chuck
  or small roast, ground
½ pound ground veal
2 tablespoons olive oil
3 cloves garlic, minced
1 large onion, chopped
1 bell pepper, chopped
¾ cup minced celery
4-ounce can
  button mushrooms
15-ounce can tomato sauce
6-ounce can tomato paste
16-ounce can plum tomatoes

1 cup water
2 to 3 teaspoons salt
2 teaspoons sugar
1 teaspoon garlic powder
1 tablespoon chili powder
1 teaspoon oregano
1 teaspoon basil
2 bay leaves
1 teaspoon cayenne pepper
¼ teaspoon cloves
1 cup red burgundy wine
  (not cooking wine)
¼ teaspoon cinnamon

Brown the ground chuck and veal in the olive oil in a heavy skillet. Add the garlic, onion, pepper, celery and mushrooms. Sauté until the onion is transparent. Add the tomato sauce, tomato paste and tomatoes with the water. Simmer for 30 minutes. Add the salt, sugar, garlic powder, chili powder, oregano, basil, bay leaves and cayenne pepper. Simmer for 2 hours until thickened. The aroma should start to make everyone hungry! Add the cloves, wine and cinnamon the last 30 minutes of cooking.

Serve over long spaghetti cooked al dente with grated Parmesan cheese. Add a tossed salad, your favorite French bread and more of the burgundy wine.

Jessi and her sister Sharon,
who is full of glee and mischief.

Country Captain

Cara Spano gave this recipe to Helen Exum with the following story: Mrs. W.L. Bullard of Columbus, Georgia, was planning to entertain Franklin Roosevelt. She wanted a very special menu to serve to her distinguished guest, so she searched her cookbooks and came up with this "now world-famous" version of Country Captain.

Soon it became the specialty at "The Big Eddy," a private club in Columbus, where many great heroes were entertained, including Generals John Pershing, George Patton, Dwight Eisenhower, Omar Bradley and George Marshall.

During World War II while en route to Europe with Fort Benning's Second Armored Division, General Patton wired the following message to Mrs. Bullard's daughter, "If you can't give me a party and have Country Captain, meet me at the train with a whole bucket of it."

1 cup flour
1 teaspoon salt
½ teaspoon pepper
4 pounds chicken breasts, split and skinned
½ cup shortening
2 onions, finely chopped
2 green peppers, chopped
1 clove garlic, minced
1 tablespoon curry
1½ teaspoons salt
½ teaspoon white pepper

Two 20-ounce cans tomatoes
½ teaspoon chopped parsley
½ teaspoon thyme
4 cups cooked long grain rice
¼ pound toasted blanched almonds
¼ cup currants
Parsley

Combine the flour, 1 teaspoon salt and pepper. Dredge the chicken in the flour mixture. Brown the chicken in the shortening in a large skillet. Remove the chicken to an ovenproof baking dish and keep warm. Sauté the onions, green peppers and garlic in the skillet until the vegetables are tender. Add the curry, 1½ teaspoons salt, white pepper, tomatoes, parsley and thyme. Bring the mixture to a boil. Pour the mixture over the chicken and bake covered at 350 degrees for 45 minutes or until the chicken is tender. Remove the chicken to a large heated platter. Pile the cooked rice around the chicken. Sprinkle the rice with the almonds and currants; garnish with the parsley. You have food for the gods.

*I cooked this recipe on the television show **Country Cooking**, with Florence Henderson. It was a big success with all of the crew.*

Pesto Cheese Cake, page 92, with a medly of fresh vegatables and fresh bread.

Kentucky Hot Brown

This is a true Kentucky recipe since it was created at the wonderful Brown Hotel in Louisville. This is one of many variations and it is a good way to use up that Thanksgiving turkey. It was on Waylon's list of favorites!

3 tablespoons butter
3 tablespoons flour
Salt and cayenne pepper
   to taste
¼ teaspoon curry, optional
1½ cups milk
¼ cup grated
   American cheese

¼ cup grated sharp
   Cheddar cheese
½ cup Parmesan cheese
8 slices turkey
4 slices bread, toasted
1 cup grated Colby
   cheese
8 slices bacon,
   nearly cooked
   or 4 thin slices
   country ham

Melt the butter in a saucepan. Add the flour, salt, cayenne pepper and curry, stirring constantly. Remove from the heat and add the milk, stirring until smooth. Return to the heat and cook slowly until thickened. Stir in the American, Cheddar and Parmesan cheeses until well blended.

Place the turkey on the toasted bread on an oven-safe baking dish. Cover with the cream sauce. Top with the Colby cheese and bacon or ham. Place the dish 6 inches under the broiler and broil slowly until the bacon or ham is cooked. Serve hot from the broiler.

Serves 4

Mexican Buffet

Shredded Beef and Bean Burritos, page 54, were Waylon's favorite.

Lorene's Enchiladas

2 pounds ground round
1 large onion, chopped
3 garlic cloves, minced
1 teaspoon salt
¼ teaspoon pepper
½ teaspoon chili powder

10-ounce can
   tomatoes with chiles
2 cups cubed
   Velveeta cheese,
   reserving ½ cup
20 corn tortillas
½ cup oil

Brown the ground round, onion and garlic in a large skillet. Add the salt, pepper, chili powder, tomatoes and cheese. Cook until the cheese melts.

Dip the corn tortillas in the hot oil for 2 to 3 seconds. Remove the tortillas and drain on paper towels. Stuff each tortilla with the meat mixture and fold the tortilla over or roll up. Place the tortillas in a 9x13-inch baking dish. Top the tortillas with the remaining ½ cup of cheese. Bake at 350 degrees for 20 minutes. Do not overcook or the tortillas will fall apart. Stuff the tortillas when ready to bake because the tortillas will crumble if made ahead of time.

Serves 10

Tennessee Chicken Enchiladas

2 chickens, cooked
2 tablespoons butter
2 medium onions,
   finely chopped
2 cloves garlic,
   finely chopped
Two 4-ounce cans
   chopped green chiles,
   drained
4-ounce can
   diced black olives, drained
½ cup chopped
   roasted red pepper
Salt and freshly-ground
   pepper to taste

12 flour tortillas
1 pound grated
   Cheddar cheese
1 pound grated
   Monterey Jack cheese
8-ounce package
   sour cream
10¾-ounce can
   cream of chicken soup
4-ounce jar pimientos
Two 14½-ounce cans
   chicken broth
2 tablespoons four
   or ¼ cup cornstarch

Remove the chicken from the bones and shred the meat. Melt the butter in a skillet and sauté the onions until they are transparent. Add the garlic, chiles, olives and red pepper. Toss in the chicken and season with the salt and pepper. Fill the tortillas evenly with the chicken mixture and top with the two cheeses. Roll the tortillas up and place in a coated 9x13-inch baking dish. Whip the sour cream and soup with a wire whisk. Add the pimientos and set aside. Pour the chicken broth into a saucepan and add the flour or cornstarch that has been dissolved in a small amount of water. Cook until the broth is thickened to the consistency of gravy. Slightly cool the mixture and gradually add the sour cream mixture. Pour this mixture over the enchiladas. Top with the remaining cheese. Bake at 325 degrees for 20 to 25 minutes or until the cheese is melted.

Shredded Beef and Bean Burritos

This is an excellent dish for parties, teenagers, football games or just as a wonderful Saturday night supper. Waylon thought these were better than any served at the finest Mexican restaurant. You can make the roast one day ahead.

6 to 8 pound shoulder
   or chuck roast
Garlic salt
Garlic powder
Lemon pepper
¼ cup canola or olive oil
14½-ounce can beef broth
4 garlic cloves
1 onion, quartered
2 cans ancho chile sauce
16-ounce can refried beans
¼ cup chopped green chiles

Flour tortillas,
   burrito style
½ pound shredded
   Colby cheese
½ pound shredded
   Monterey Jack cheese
Chopped tomatoes
Chopped onion
Salsa
Shredded lettuce
Avocado slices
1 teaspoon each
   Cumin and Chili Powder

Season the roast generously with the garlic salt, garlic powder and lemon pepper. Pour the oil into a Dutch oven and heat. Sear the roast, browning the seasonings to form a crust on the roast. Season very heavily for a nice crust that will hold juices in.

Add the beef broth and enough water to cover ⅔ of the roast. Add the garlic and onion. Bake at 500 degrees for 15 minutes. Reduce the heat to 300 degrees and cook for 4 hours or until the roast is falling apart and can be shredded easily.

Remove the roast from the broth and cool. Strain the broth and reserve. Shred the roast and place it in a large skillet. Add the ancho chile sauce, **cumin, chili powder,** refried beans, green chiles and enough of the reserved broth to barely cover the meat. Simmer until the sauce is a thick gravy.

Heat the tortillas 30 minutes before serving; the tortillas should be soft and easy to work with. Place ½ cup of the beef mixture in the middle of each tortilla and top the meat with the cheeses. Fold the sides and roll to form a burrito.

Place the burritos in two coated 9x13-inch baking dishes and top with extra cheese. Cover and heat for 15 to 20 minutes until the cheese is melted. Garnish with the chopped tomatoes, onion, salsa, lettuce and avocado slices. Serve with cooked rice.

Serves 12

Maureen's Chicken Fajitas

2 pounds chicken tenders
  cut into bite-size pieces or strips
2 green peppers, cut into strips
2 onions, cut into strips
White pepper
Cracked black pepper
Garlic salt
Dash of salt
Dash of garlic powder
2 tablespoons olive oil

Allegro Marinade
½ cup peanut oil
8 flour tortillas
16-ounce can
  refried beans
Salsa
Sour cream
Grated cheese
Jalapeños, sliced

Allegro Marinade is a mixture of soy sauce, lemon juice and lime juice.

Place the chicken, green peppers and onions in a large baking dish. Sprinkle generously with the white pepper, black pepper, garlic salt, salt and garlic powder.

Combine the olive oil and Allegro Marinade. Add the mixture to the chicken. Marinate the chicken, covered and chilled, for 5 to 6 hours. Stir fry the mixture on high in small batches until lightly browned in the peanut oil.

Warm the flour tortillas in foil at 300 degrees for 30 minutes along with the refried beans. Serve on a cast-iron sizzling grill plate. Garnish with the salsa, sour cream, grated cheese and jalapeños.

Mexican Rice

1 box basmati rice	Chicken broth
1 tablespoon butter	1 cup chopped onion
2 tablespoons olive oil	¼ cup cilantro
1 cup baby niblet corn	1 cup chopped parsley
or Shoe Peg corn	Cracked black pepper

Brown the rice in the butter and olive oil until the rice is a light golden brown. Remove the rice to an 8-inch baking dish. Stir in the corn and enough of the chicken broth to barely cover the rice. Add the onion to the skillet and sauté until the onion is transparent. Add the onion to the rice mixture.

Bake at 325 degrees until the rice is fluffy and has absorbed the broth. Stir in the cilantro and parsley and bake for 15 minutes. Remove the rice from the oven and add the cracked pepper. Serve with burritos.

Tamale Pie

6 boneless chicken breasts
1 large onion, chopped
1 large green bell pepper,
  chopped
1 tablespoon butter
1½ teaspoons chili powder
1 teaspoon garlic salt
1 teaspoon cumin
10¾-ounce can
  cream of chicken soup

10¾-ounce can
  cream of
  mushroom soup
10-ounce can tomatoes
  with green chiles
½ pound light
  Cheddar or
  Colby cheese
16-ounce bag white
  restaurant-style
  tortilla chips

We particularly loved this dish and it was a favorite on football days. Coupled with a big green salad Tamale Pie will satisfy the heartiest appetite. Your guests will like it made with chicken, but they will rave about it when made with beef.

Boil the chicken for 25 minutes or until tender. Cool and cut into bite-size cubes. Set the chicken aside. Sauté the onion and pepper in the butter. Add the chili powder, garlic salt, cumin, cream of chicken soup, cream of mushroom soup and tomatoes; mix well. Add ½ of the cheese to the onion mixture and cook until the cheese melts.

Layer the tortilla chips, ½ of the chicken and ½ of the cheese sauce in a coated 9x13-inch baking dish. Repeat a second time. Top the mixture with the remaining tortilla chips. Sprinkle the remaining cheese on top. Cover and bake at 375 degrees for 30 minutes.

Serves 8 to 10

Ground sirloin can also be used. Brown the sirloin and drain.

Red Snapper with Green Pepper Corn Sauce

4 red snapper fillets,
   skinned and boned
½ cup flour
½ cup butter
¼ cup chicken stock

¾ cup heavy cream
2 fresh tarragon leaves
   or ¼ teaspoon dried
3 ounces green pepper
   corn sauce
Salt to taste

Dredge the fillets in the flour. Melt the butter in a large skillet. Sauté the fillets, turning carefully with a spatula to avoid breaking them. When nicely browned, add the the chicken stock, cream, tarragon, green pepper corn sauce and salt. Cook over a low heat until the liquid is reduced or bake at 350 degrees for 10 minutes.

Barbecued Pork Chops

18 thin pork chops
3 tablespoons olive oil
White wine vinegar
Lemon juice
Soy sauce

Salt and pepper to taste
1 bottle Waylon's
   barbecue sauce
   or your favorite sauce

Scrape and trim any excess fat from the pork chops. Arrange the pork chops in a baking dish. Baste both sides of the pork chops with the olive oil. Shake the vinegar and squeeze the lemon juice over the chops. Add several dashes of the soy sauce, salt and pepper. Refrigerate for 2 to 6 hours to marinate. Place the chops on a baking sheet and pour the marinade over the pork chops. Bake at 325 degrees for 2 hours. Remove the chops from the marinade and place them on a platter. Generously baste the chops with the barbecue sauce.

Grill the chops for 5 to 7 minutes on each side. This will dry the sauce out since the pork chops are done when they come out of the oven.

Serves 6 allowing 3 thin pork chops per person

Chicken Cordon Bleu

8 slices cooked ham
8 slices Swiss cheese
8 whole boneless
    chicken breast fillets, flattened
3 tablespoons minced parsley

Pepper to taste
1 egg, beaten
½ cup bread crumbs
¼ cup butter

Place 1 slice of the ham and 1 slice of the cheese in the center of each piece of chicken. Sprinkle the chicken with the parsley and pepper. Roll up each chicken breast lengthwise and secure with a wooden pick. Dip each piece of the chicken into the beaten egg. Dredge the chicken in the bread crumbs, coating well.

Melt the butter in a heavy skillet and brown the chicken. Place the chicken in a 9x13-inch baking dish. Bake uncovered at 350 degrees for 40 to 45 minutes.

Serves 8

Lazy Man's Ribs and Just Slaw

Russell and Mary Mann helped us care for Shooter as god-grandparents and supervised our home for many years. They both retired from military careers. Mary trained most good doctors when she ran surgical intensive care at Veterans Hospital in Nashville. She always checked on us if we were ill and they often joined us on family outings.

This is one of our fondest memories.

We started at 7:38 a.m. that icy morning, with snow still on the ground and icicles melting slowly. You've not lived until you've been in a Southern ice storm.

Russell brought his roasting pan large enough to hold 14 pounds of baby-back pork spareribs. He seasoned them with chili-powder and black pepper using a strong right arm. Then he doused them with a good red wine vinegar. He placed the ribs in the roasting pan with lemon wedges and added big cans of tomatoes as well as 2 quartered onions. He preheated the oven to 350 degrees, then lowered it to 300 degrees and let the mixture cook for 1 ½ hours to permeate the meat with flavor before he began to barbecue.

Outside on the smoke side of the grill, Russell stacked 12 pounds of charcoal so the heat and smoke would cover the meat while grilling and dry out the very wet ribs. He placed hickory-bark (mesquite and applewood optional) near the charcoal but not close enough to ignite–just char and smoke. Soak the bark in water for 5 minutes to prevent igniting the wood.

Russell turned the ribs in the oven, then he lit the charcoal. He judged the sky while he waited until the smell of igniter was gone. While the ribs were finishing in the oven and the coals were burning, Mary shredded a head of cabbage for "Just Slaw." Maureen commented that she'd never seen that type of slaw. Mary said, "This is from South Carolina, that's why you'll need 3 tablespoons chopped onion, tomato and mayonnaise to taste along with sweet pickles and that's all."

At 9:15 a.m. we placed the ribs on the grill on the shelf above the charcoal. I seared 2 pounds boneless, skinless chicken breasts on a separate grill on medium heat to seal the juices. Then I brushed each breast generously with Waylon's Barbecue Sauce. About every 11 minutes I brushed the breasts again and removed them when they were done. We cooked the chicken at least 30 minutes. We basted the ribs less often than the chicken and took both the ribs and chicken off around 10:30; covered them with foil; and placed them in warm oven with 2 large loaves of Hawaiian bread.

Lazy Man's Ribs and Just Slaw were prepared and served for a luncheon at Southern Comfort for a film crew working there with Waylon. They dubbed the meal a huge success. We still try to recreate Russell and Mary's recipes today. Sadly, they have since passed away but their devotion to us and the memories we made are very much alive.

Fried Chicken

2 to 3 pieces chicken per person
2 cups milk
2 eggs
2 cups flour

2 teaspoons salt
1 teaspoon pepper
½ teaspoon paprika
Shortening

Soak the chicken parts in a bowl of salted water for a few hours or overnight in the refrigerator. Remove the chicken from the water and dry on paper towels. Combine the milk and eggs in a bowl and beat well. Combine the flour, salt, pepper and paprika in a shallow bowl.

Melt the shortening in an iron skillet to 1 inch deep. Dip the chicken in the milk mixture and dredge in the flour mixture. Place the chicken in the hot skillet, about 4 to 5 pieces at a time. Turn the heat down to medium when the chicken begins to brown. Cover and cook slowly turning the chicken a couple of times. Cook for 20 to 30 minutes. Remove the cover and return to high heat the last 5 minutes to crisp. Remove the chicken and drain on paper towels. Serve the chicken hot, warm, room temperature or cold. It is good anyway you serve it. We like only the breasts and legs, so that is all we fry.

Marie's Macaroni Salad

16-ounce box bite-size
   elbow macaroni
8-ounce jar
   sweet midget pickles, chopped
3 hard-boiled eggs, chopped
2 cups chopped celery
1 cup chopped onion
1 cup chopped cucumber

½ cup finely-chopped
   radishes
1½ cups mayonnaise
Salt and
   white pepper to taste
Paprika
Parsley, chopped
Tomato wedges

Cook the macaroni according to the package directions. Rinse and cool the macaroni. Add the pickles, eggs, celery, onion, cucumber, radishes, mayonnaise, salt and pepper; mix well. Garnish with the paprika, parsley and tomato wedges.

Serves 10 to 12

Potato Salad

10 large white potatoes
½ cup sour cream
2 cups mayonnaise
2 hard-boiled eggs, chopped
2 tablespoons vinegar
Dash of yellow mustard
2 tablespoons hot-sweet mustard
2 cups finely-diced celery

½ cup finely-diced onion
¼ cup finely-diced
   green pepper
½ cup finely-diced
   sweet pickles
Salt, pepper and
   Tabasco sauce to taste

Boil the potatoes in their skins. Cool the potatoes and remove the skins. Cut the potatoes into bite-size pieces. Combine the sour cream, mayonnaise, eggs, vinegar, mustards, celery, onion, green pepper, pickles, salt, pepper and Tabasco sauce; mix well. Add the potatoes and mix well.

Serves 12

Use light mayonnaise and sour cream to reduce the fat.

Rice and Cauliflower Salad

1 cup instant rice
Two 8-ounce cans shrimp
1 green pepper, chopped
1 onion, chopped
2 cups cauliflower florets
½ cup pimento-stuffed olives,
    sliced

Juice of 1 lemon
¼ teaspoon
    Tabasco sauce
½ teaspoon salt
¼ teaspoon pepper
½ cup mayonnaise

This recipe can be doubled or tripled for large occasions. It keeps well and can be made ahead. This salad is great for cookouts and barbecues. One of Waylon's favorites!

Cook the rice according to the package directions. Combine the rice, shrimp, pepper, onion, cauliflower, olives, lemon juice, Tabasco sauce, salt, pepper and mayonnaise.

Laura's Summer Chicken Salad

This was a favorite of the Nashville songwriters. Waylon was famous for his songwriters lunches.

3 pounds chicken breasts,
  cooked and diced
½ cup diced yellow bell pepper
½ cup diced red bell pepper
1 cup diced purple onion
2 cups diced celery
½ teaspoon curry powder
½ teaspoon salt
¼ teaspoon pepper

1 cup chopped pecans
¼ cup chicken broth
½ to 1 cup mayonnaise
1 head Boston lettuce,
  separated
16-ounce can
  mandarin oranges
1 bunch red seedless
  grapes

Combine the chicken, peppers, onion, celery, curry powder, salt, pepper, pecans and chicken broth; mix well. Fold in the mayonnaise. Cover and chill. Arrange the lettuce on salad plates. Pile the chicken salad on the lettuce. Garnish with the mandarin oranges and grapes. Serve with Yellow Squash Muffins.

Yellow Squash Muffins

6 to 8 yellow squash
2 eggs
1 stick butter, melted
1 cup sugar

3 cups flour
1 tablespoon plus
  2 teaspoons
  baking powder
1 teaspoon salt

Cut the squash into 1-inch slices. Place the squash in a saucepan and add water to cover. Cook for 15 to 20 minutes, drain and mash. Combine the squash, eggs and butter and stir well. Combine the sugar, flour, baking powder and salt. Add the squash mixture, stirring just until moistened. Spoon the batter into coated muffin cups. Bake at 375 degrees for 20 minutes.

Makes 18 muffins

Spinach Salad with Chutney Dressing

2 pounds fresh spinach
8 ounces fresh mushrooms, sliced
2 red onions, sliced and separated into rings
2 cloves garlic
½ cup olive oil
2 teaspoons Dijon mustard
¼ teaspoon salt
¼ cup raspberry wine vinegar
3 tablespoons chutney
2 teaspoons sugar
¼ teaspoon pepper
6 ounces crisp bacon, crumbled
Freshly-ground pepper

Wash the spinach in water to remove any sand. Trim off and discard tough stems or bruised leaves. Drain and shake off any excess water and pat dry with a paper towel. Tear or cut the spinach into bite-size pieces. Add the mushrooms and onions.

Marinate the garlic in the olive oil for 1 hour or longer. Remove the garlic to a bowl and add the mustard, salt, vinegar, chutney, sugar and pepper; mixing well.

Toss the spinach mixture with the chutney mixture when ready to serve. Add the bacon and a generous amount of the freshly-ground pepper.

Mary Cox's Spinach Salad

2 pounds fresh spinach,
  washed and torn
  into bite-size pieces
8-ounce can
  sliced water chestnuts
8 large mushrooms,
  thinly sliced
½ cup sugar
1 cup canola or olive oil
⅓ cup ketchup

½ cup vinegar
2 tablespoons
  Worcestershire sauce
2 tablespoons
  minced onion
4 hard-boiled eggs,
  chopped
10 slices bacon,
  cooked crisp
  and crumbled

Combine the spinach, water chestnuts and mushrooms. Combine the sugar, oil, ketchup, vinegar, Worcestershire sauce and onion. Shake well. Add the dressing to the spinach mixture and toss to coat. Add the eggs and bacon and serve.

This was a favorite of Waylon's and many enjoyed this at his famous songwriters lunches.

Cream of Mushroom Soup

1 pound fresh mushrooms
¼ cup butter
¼ cup flour
1½ quarts chicken broth

2 cups light cream
¼ teaspoon thyme
Pinch of cayenne pepper
Salt to taste

Wipe the mushrooms clean with a moist paper towel; remove the stems. Melt the butter in a large saucepan. Add the flour gradually, stirring to make a paste. Add 1 cup of the broth and stir until slightly thickened. Add the remaining broth and bring to a boil, stirring occasionally. Reduce the heat and simmer for 4 to 5 minutes.

Chop the mushrooms and purée in a blender container or food processor using a small amount of the chicken broth. Add the mushroom purée to the saucepan. Stir in the cream. Season with the thyme, cayenne pepper and salt. Simmer for 4 to 5 minutes.

Serves 8 to 10

Secret: Place the soup in a large pan of hot water to keep warm or to reheat. Do not place the soup over direct heat. Add a small amount of cream before reheating.

Old-Fashioned Cream of Tomato Soup

1 stick butter
½ cup flour
Dash of Tabasco sauce
4 cups milk
1½ cups prepared
    Bloody Mary mix
2½ pounds diced tomatoes

1½ cups tomato juice
½ cup sugar
2 cups heavy cream
2½ teaspoons salt
2 teaspoons pepper
Sour cream
Green onions, chopped

Combine the butter and flour to make a roux in a large pot. Add the Tabasco sauce. Be careful not to brown the roux. Add the milk, Bloody Mary mix, tomatoes, tomato juice, sugar, cream, salt and pepper. Simmer for 15 minutes. Garnish each serving with a dollop of the sour cream and green onions.

Vegetable Soup

If you sauté the vegetables before putting them into the stock, the soup will taste better. Your family will notice the difference if you take the extra time.

Note: When you cook the macaroni separately, you do not get soft mushy, over-cooked pasta as you do when you put the macaroni directly in the soup. I have also found that putting the macaroni in the soup to cook acts like a sponge soaking away all of the stock.

3 pounds round soupbones
8 cups hot water
3 cups tomato juice
2 to 3 teaspoons salt
2 tablespoons
   Worcestershire sauce
½ teaspoon chili powder
2 bay leaves
1 pound top round, cubed
16-ounce can diced tomatoes

2 cups celery
10-ounce package
   frozen corn
1 cup sliced carrots
10-ounce package
   frozen lima beans
2 cups diced potatoes
½ cup chopped onion
16-ounce box bite-size
   elbow macaroni

Sear the bones in a 5-quart saucepan or Dutch oven on very high heat. Turn the bones often to keep from burning. Pour the water over the soupbones after the soupbones are browned and reduce the heat. Add the tomato juice, salt, Worcestershire sauce, chili powder and bay leaves. Cover and simmer for 3 hours. Remove the bones and discard. Refrigerate the stock for several hours or overnight until the fat rises to the top. Skim the fat and return the stock to the stove. Coat the top round in salt and pepper and brown in a small amount of oil. Add the top round and cook for 1½ hours. Add the tomatoes, celery, corn, carrots, limas, potatoes and onion and simmer for 1 hour uncovered until the meat is tender.

Prepare the macaroni according the package directions to the al dente stage. Drain the macaroni and cool. Place ½ to 1 cup cooked macaroni in a bowl. Pour the hot soup over the macaroni and serve.

Serves 8

Beef Stew

2 pounds lean top round steak,
  cut into bite-size chunks
1 teaspoon salt
¼ teaspoon pepper
3 tablespoons flour
2 tablespoons canola oil

6 to 8 carrots,
  cut into 2-inch chunks
1 cup chopped onion
2 tablespoons
  tomato paste
1½ cups chicken broth

Rub the steak with the salt and pepper. Dredge the meat in the flour. Brown the meat in the canola oil in a large Dutch oven over medium-high heat.

Sauté the carrots and onion in a skillet. Add the sautéed vegetables to the meat. Add the tomato paste and chicken broth. Simmer for 2 to 3 hours. Stir often and add broth if needed. Thicken the sauce with cornstarch and water, if the sauce is not thick like gravy. Correct the seasonings.

Serves 6

A good stew is at its best when served over mashed potatoes, however, noodles and rice are also good. The secret here is to sauté the vegetables before adding them to the stew. This brings out the flavor before adding them to the pot. Also, using chicken broth instead of water makes a big difference. When made with water, people will eat it, but when made with chicken broth, they will rave about it!

Baked Stuffed Yellow Squash

A dish similar to this was served in grander days at one of Kentucky's oldest inns, Old Stone Inn, in Simpsonville. This is so complete, it can be used as an entrée.

Note: Zucchini squash also works very well with this. This recipe was given to us by Paul Stanley, an excellent Kentucky chef.

6 small yellow squash
¾ pound pork or
  turkey sausage
½ cup chopped onion
2 tablespoons
  chopped parsley
3-ounce can
  sliced mushrooms
¾ cup cooked rice

1 tablespoon butter
1 clove garlic
2 cups tomatoes
2 teaspoons sugar
2 tablespoons butter
½ cup butter
  cracker crumbs
Parsley

Cook the squash in boiling water for 10 minutes or until tender. Cut a thin slice off the side of each squash and scoop out the pulp leaving ½ inch of squash all around. Mash the pulp and seeds and set aside. Lightly salt the inside of the shells. Brown the sausage in a skillet and drain. Add the onion, parsley, mushrooms and the squash pulp. Sauté until the onion is tender. Add the rice; mix well. Fill each squash shell with the rice-sausage mixture.

Melt the 1 tablespoon of butter in a saucepan. Sauté the garlic and add the tomatoes and sugar. Mash the tomatoes and cook until you have a nice thick sauce. Spoon the tomato sauce on top of the rice-sausage mixture. Melt the 2 tablespoons of butter in a saucepan. Add the cracker crumbs and stir until lightly browned. Sprinkle the crumbs on top of the tomato sauce. Bake at 375 degrees for 30 minutes or until heated through. Sprinkle with the parsley and you will have a spectacular dish.

Butter Rich Mashed Potatoes

2 quarts water
1 teaspoon salt
6 to 8 large potatoes,
    peeled and quartered

1 cup butter
1 cup whipping cream
Salt and white pepper
    to taste

Pour the water into a 4 to 5-quart saucepan or Dutch oven. Add the salt and bring to a boil. Add the potatoes and cook, covered, for 20 to 25 minutes. Drain and cover the pot with a towel for 5 minutes. This will make the potatoes meaty. Shake the pot well, remove the cloth and mash the potatoes. Add the butter and continue to mash. Pour in the cream slowly and beat the potatoes using an electric mixer. Use more or less cream as the size of potatoes vary. Season with the salt and white pepper. These are the best mashed potatoes you will ever eat.

Serves 8 to 10

Eula Pickett's Squash Casserole

½ stick butter
4 tablespoons flour
1 cup chopped onion
2 cups milk
2 cups grated cheese

½ stick butter
  or margarine
2 cups cracker crumbs
2 cups cubed,
  cooked squash

Melt the ½ stick of butter in a saucepan. Add the flour and onion. Add the milk and cheese and cook until thick.

Melt the ½ stick of butter and mix in the cracker crumbs. Layer the squash, sauce and cracker crumbs in a baking dish. Bake at 350 degrees for 40 minutes.

Serves 8

Fried Okra

1 cup cornmeal
1 teaspoon salt
½ teaspoon pepper

3 to 4 cups okra,
  sliced in ¼-inch slices
⅓ cup oil
  or bacon drippings

Place the cornmeal, salt and pepper in a resealable plastic bag and add the okra. Shake to coat. Empty the okra into a colander and shake off the excess cornmeal. Heat the oil or bacon drippings in a heavy skillet. Add the okra and cook on high for 3 to 4 minutes. Stir and turn; reduce the heat to medium low, frying slowly, stirring often to prevent sticking. Cook for 20 to 30 minutes until the okra is a rich dark brown. Return the heat to high the last 5 minutes. Okra prepared this way will be crunchy on the outside and tender on the inside.

Russell's Zucchini Casserole

8 small zucchini, cubed
2 tablespoons butter
1 medium onion, chopped
10¾-ounce can
   cream of mushroom soup
½ tablespoon sugar
2 eggs, beaten
½ cup chopped almonds

1 cup grated Cheddar
   or Colby cheese
½ cup butter, melted
1½ cups butter crackers,
   crumbled
1 teaspoon salt
¼ teaspoon pepper

Cover the zucchini with water in a saucepan and bring to a boil. Cook for 5 minutes and drain. Set the zucchini aside.

Melt the 2 tablespoons of butter in a skillet. Sauté the onion until it is tender. Add the zucchini, soup, sugar, eggs, almonds and cheese. Pour the mixture into a 9-inch square baking dish. Melt the ½ cup butter in a skillet and stir in the cracker crumbs. Toss until the crumbs are lightly browned. Top the zucchini mixture with the crackers and bake at 350 degrees for 25 minutes.

Serves 6

Russell Mann was a friend and loyal employee for many years. He loved to raise a garden and often said, "Zucchini are so easy to grow, they would even grow on a rock!" He often had more of this green monster than he knew what to do with and being a fine cook, he would invent ways of using it. This casserole was one of his best.

Stuffed Baked Potatoes

This recipe has always been a favorite among the Jennings children. It is so sinfully rich, we seldom prepare it these days. However, on birthdays, holidays, and special events, we give in to the requests and make these delicious potatoes.

10 large baking potatoes
1 pound Colby cheese, grated
1 cup butter
16 ounces bacon, cooked crisp and crumbled
1 cup heavy whipping cream
Salt and pepper to taste

Scrub the potatoes and pat dry with paper towels. Rub the potato skins with olive oil and poke a few holes in the potatoes with the tines of a fork. Place the potatoes directly on the oven rack and bake at 500 degrees for 1 hour. Remove the potatoes from the oven and cut a small slice off of the top. Do not cut in half.

Scoop the potato pulp into a big bowl and mash well. Add the cheese, butter, bacon, cream and salt and pepper. Beat the mixture with an electric mixer until smooth. Fill the potato shell with a heaping amount of the pulp mixture, filling well above the shell. Place the potatoes on a baking sheet and bake at 400 degrees for 20 minutes until they begin to brown and form a crust.

Stuffed Zucchini Boats

6 small to medium zucchini
1 tablespoon butter
1 tablespoon sugar
8 ounces shredded
  Colby cheese

6 finely-sliced
  green onions
2 tablespoons diced
  jalapeño peppers
  or 1 tablespoon fresh
¼ to ½ cup mayonnaise

Wash the zucchini and trim off the ends. Place the zucchini in a 5-quart saucepan or Dutch oven with boiling, salted water. Cover and cook for 8 to 10 minutes, until the zucchini are tender but not completely done. Cut a small slice off the side of each of the zucchini. Scoop the pulp out and pat the inside dry. Place a dot of the butter and a ½ teaspoon of the sugar in each zucchini boat. Place the zucchini in a baking dish.

Combine the cheese, onions, jalapeños and mayonnaise in a bowl and mix well. Spoon the cheese mixture into the zucchini boats. Bake uncovered at 350 degrees for 20 to 25 minutes or until the cheese is melted.

Serves 6

Friends and Entertaining

Southern Comfort stands near the road frequently traveled by Andrew Jackson when he visited a friend's farm known as "Cold Saturday" in the township of Brentwood, Tennessee. Many a weary traveler has been refreshed and renewed while dining and exchanging stories with good friends in the lush, green rolling hills south of Nashville. For those who travel for a living, as we have done, returning to your homeplace is the only true way to rest and revitalize your energies. Perhaps a home means more after you've been away from it. King Solomon tells us that a man away from home is like a bird away from its nest, and we agree. We named our home Southern Comfort because it's the place where our hearts grow lighter after a weary journey.

Johnny Cash's Party

Johnny Cash needed a party to celebrate his new-found sobriety after another bout with drug addiction. His wife, June Carter Cash, had just given a party for Waylon in their mansion on Old Hickory Lake, so we decided to celebrate our good friend in a style that would befit the Rock-a-Billy King of the South. I began planning a party with a fifties theme and as much like a "picnic on the grounds" as I could.

Maureen and I, along with the help of Dianne Keenen and her entertaining company, An Affair to Remember, developed a strategy. Waylon and I would dress in our prom regalia. Mine was my lifelong favorite, a strapless dress with yellow netting. Waylon would wear his tuxedo. Our front yard was adorned with a tent. Lilacs were chosen for the party and we began to set up round tables draped in white tablecloths with white garden chairs. The sun was shining just for Johnny that day.

"teenaged" queen, wore her aqua taffeta and lace gown that fell way above her knees.

Kris and Lisa Kristofferson with their first-born, Jesse, were surprise guests who flew in from the west coast to join us.

Robert Duvall and his wife, Gail, were dressed as Johnny and June (Bob as June, Gail as John). He would later do a scathing roast of the two guests of honor.

Willie Nelson and his tall blonde wife, Connie, were there. Only Willie's sunglasses, with mini-windshield wipers, detracted from his ability

Jessi and Waylon dressed for the Fifties at Johnny Cash's party

Jessi and June Carter Cash are joined by Paula and Connie Nelson

He arrived wearing jeans, a T-shirt with a pack of cigarettes rolled up in the sleeve and a grin like a teenager. June, his

to float like a cloud from room to room with that irresistible smile.

Hank and Becky Williams were also part of the group. Hank is a natural comic and he and Willie started telling stories as soon as they found each other.

Jim Varney, best known as "Vern" in movies, arrived with a skit called "Mistake" that fascinated everyone. John Jay Hooker gave his big hat to Johnny after repeating his father's saying that putting on a hat when you enter a difficult situation allows you to handle it.

After eating a fine Southern meal, we drifted into the living room to offer Johnny special gifts. Among them were a song by Kris Kristofferson titled "Good Morning, John" and a saxophone solo by Donna Spence. John's manager, Lou Robbin, gave our hand-carved eagle to John as a stand-in gift of his own. Waylon presented John with a rifle. Paula Lovell Hooker, wearing her felt poodle skirt with a crinoline slip and oxfords, danced a mighty fine jitterbug with her dance partner just for Johnny. What a time we had!

Rodney Crowell sings a song for John.

Good Ole' Boys at Johnny Cash's party.

MENU

Asparagus Finger Sandwiches
Fried Chicken
Ham
Green Beans
Corn Bread
Fresh Melon and Fruits
Fresh Corn
Biscuits
Rice Casserole
Individual Ice Cream Sundaes

Scenes from Johnny Cash's party.

More friends that helped us celebrate.

Willie and Hank looked a little too serious!

*Paula Lovell shows off her jitterbug skills
with her dance partner at the Fifties party.*

East and West Meets South

From time to time we like to take out our fine silver service for breakfast and this special business meeting was just such an occasion. So, we decided to treat them to some really famous Southern dishes.

We had a buffet of Tennessee country ham and red-eye gravy, cheese grits, homemade Angel biscuits with assorted jams, eggs scrambled with a delicate cheese sauce, homemade sausage patties and sausage gravy. It was quite amusing to watch the men question what each dish was. Before the meal was over, they were begging for the recipes. Our guest's usual breakfasts were either fresh fruit or cereal. They were so well fed from this meal, that it took several pots of coffee to keep them awake to complete their business meeting.

Wildcat Party

The year before the Kentucky Wildcats came to dinner, Waylon had taken Shooter to Atlanta to the NCAA Tournament. During the tournament, Waylon got to know Coach Eddie Sutton from the University of Kentucky. His new-found friendship prompted him to invite the entire team, staff and coach to dinner the next year when they came to Nashville. This was one invitation that was not forgotten. A few weeks before the scheduled game with Vanderbilt, Coach Sutton called to see if the invitation was still on.

It was time for the "elves" to begin to pull this together. We knew the decor called for blue and white, and the food had to be a hearty affair. Tables were placed in every room at Southern Comfort and they were all decorated in the school colors, from the tablecloths to the flowers.

We hosted fifty people that night and the buffet was abundant. Many whole tenderloins of beef roasted to perfection were prepared, as well as huge hams glazed and sliced, and tons of barbecue ribs that were donated and flown in from the Montgomery Inn in Northern Kentucky.

Next came big dishes of baked beans, scalloped potatoes, an array of salads, homemade breads and vegetables. We learned a valuable lesson that night, seven foot basketball players don't like salads or vegetables. They like meat and bread. Those tenderloins disappeared in a flash. Some of

The Kentucky Wildcats eat heartily from Maureen's buffet.

The Kentucky Wildcats party.

Whole Tenderloin, Baked
Cremated Ham with Glaze
Montgomery Inn Ribs
Three-Bean Baked Beans
Macaroni Salad - Potato Salad
Scalloped Potatoes
Broccoli Casserole
Relish Tray
Homemade Rolls
Pecan Pie

the young men asked for ketchup to go on the meat. Now, one doesn't refuse anything when asked by a 6 foot, 10-inch, 240-pound person.

We always thought we had a large home with high ceilings but that night, the Wildcats definitely filled it to the top. It's hard to believe how massive the players are when you see them on the basketball court. Bring them into your home and you'll notice very quickly.

It was a wonderful evening. We sang for the team and they played and sang their music for us, too.

The next day, we attended the game and the Wildcats suffered a devastating loss—one of the worst on record. Maureen was sure it had been her cooking that caused them to play so badly.

Chet and The Boys

Chet Atkins has a been part of our life for a long time and was the first person to appreciate my song writing. He placed my music with artists he produced in the 60's such as Dottie West, Hank Locklin, Don Gibson, etc. He brought Waylon from Phoenix, Arizona to Nashville and helped launch his place in the music industry. Chet watched over Roger Miller's progress, was deeply concerned for Don Gibson's health and worried that Waylon was going to stay in trouble forever. So, I thought he deserved a party. I wanted a small gathering where all three of his superstars were united and they had an opportunity to show him their "well-being."

Leona Atkins' Pintos and Corn Bread

16-ounce package pinto beans   Salt pork
8 cups water

You may want to play your favorite Chet Atkins album while the beans are simmering.

P.S. Chet didn't like Jessi's corn bread. He said it tasted like cake.

Rinse the pinto beans and remove the rocks. Ass the water and soak the beans in a large saucepan overnight.

Drain the beans, replace the water and add the salt pork. Bring the water to a boil. Turn off the heat and allow to stand for 1 hour. Return to the heat and simmer for 2 hours. Serve with Old-Fashioned Plain Corn Bread, sliced tomatoes and chilled sliced onions. Don't forget the iced tea!

I suggested a Southern dinner of corn bread, beans and summer vegetables. I rounded up the pillars of progressive country music and together we honored Chet with good stories and great moments in time. After we "broke bread" we moved into the living room where Roger Miller began telling Don Gibson how he stole "Don Gibson" licks off songs to write "Lock Stock and Teardrops." Waylon played his version for Roger, which Roger had not heard, and they all laughed. Roger sang parts of his songs that reminded him of Don's phrasing in hits like "I Can t Stop Loving You," "Sweet Dreams," "Old Lonesome Me," etc. Chet had been recording Mark Knopfler of "Dire Straits" instrumentally and Mark chimed in with a beautiful number of his own. Don Gibson remained pretty quiet except for appreciating everyone else's vocal and instrumental contributions. Then for a moment, time rolled back to the 60's and it seemed a life came into Don. He sang "I Can't Stop Loving You" for us with all the heart and soul we remembered him having. He's remained incognito for a number of years and fought his own battle through bypass surgery. No one has seen much of him or his lovely wife, Bobbi, but he telephones Chet occasionally.

If Roger and Mary Miller had not had to leave to tend to their daughter, Taylor, I don't think any of us would have been able to pull away from each other. Chet is not the only one who'll never forget that night.

Plain Old-Fashioned Corn Bread

2 cups self-rising cornmeal   1¾ cups buttermilk
1 egg   ¼ cup melted shortening

Combine the cornmeal, egg, buttermilk and shortening. Pour the batter into a hot coated iron skillet. Bake at 450 degrees for 20 to 25 minutes.

A Typical Week at Southern Comfort

Birthday Celebration
Marie's Chili
Hot Rolls
Eight-Layer Mexican Dip
Baked Tortilla Chips with Salsa
Iced Tea
Cake and Ice Cream

Lunch with Film Industry Guests From LA
Grilled Salmon with Dill Sauce
Spinach Salad with Chutney Dressing
Braised Carrots and Brussels Sprouts
Wild Rice Pilaf with Vegetables
Refrigerator Rolls
Poached Pears with Semisweet Chocolate Sauce
Macadamia Nut Dessert Coffee

RCA Lunch: Listening to Waylon's New Album
Salmon Salad
Tortellini Soup
Italian Country Bread
Poached Pears with Crème Anglaise
Iced Tea with Mint

Super Bowl Day
Skinny Spinach Dip with Raw Vegetables
Tuna Pâte with Crackers and Sourdough Bread
Fruit Crackers
Chutney Cheese Caper with Strawberries and Pineapple Skewers
Fruit Bread
Eight-Layer Mexican Dip
Hot and Sour Soup with Lemon Grass
Rice Noodles with Vegetables
Shrimp with Noodles
Pork with Vegetables
Chocolate Cake
Coconut Pound Cake

Chili Dip

1 pound ground round
1 pound American Cheese,
  cubed
10-ounce can
  green chiles and tomatoes

2 teaspoons
  Worcestershire sauce
½ teaspoon
  chili powder

This is a wonderful dish to serve while your guests are watching big sporting events. Men especially love it.

Brown the ground round in a skillet until done throughout. Add the cheese, green chiles and tomatoes, Worcestershire sauce and chili powder and mix well. Cover and simmer for 1 hour.

Serve with corn chips or Doritos. Serve in a fondue pot to keep it warm.

Eight-Layer Mexican Dip

Two 10½-ounce cans
  jalapeño bean dip
2 to 3 avocados,
  peeled and mashed
2 tablespoons lemon juice
Dash of salt and pepper
Dash of Tabasco sauce
Two 1.25-ounce packages
  taco seasoning
½ cup mayonnaise
1 cup sour cream

1 large bunch
  green onions, chopped
3 medium tomatoes,
  chopped
14-ounce can ripe olives,
  drained and chopped
½ pound
  Monterey Jack or
  sharp Cheddar cheese,
  grated
4 ounces picante sauce

Layer the bean dip in the bottom of a large glass bowl or baking dish. Combine the avocados, lemon juice, salt, pepper and Tabasco sauce in a small bowl and mix well. Layer the avocado mixture on top of the bean dip. Combine the taco seasoning, mayonnaise and sour cream in a small bowl and mix well. Layer the sour cream mixture on top of the avocado mixture. Layer the green onions on top of the sour cream mixture. Layer the tomatoes, olives and cheese. Make a well in the center for the picante sauce. Serve with tostada chips.

Serves 14 to 20

Water Chestnuts with Hot Mustard Sauce

1 cup dry mustard
1 cup apple cider vinegar
6 eggs
2 cups sugar
Dash of salt

Four 8-ounce cans
    water chestnuts
1 pound thin bacon,
    sliced in half
Vegetable oil

Combine the dry mustard and vinegar in a small bowl. Cover and refrigerate overnight.

Place the mustard sauce in a saucepan and add the eggs, sugar and salt. Cook over a medium heat for 10 minutes and beat with an electric mixer until the mixture is thickened. Remove from the heat and allow the mixture to cool.

Wrap each water chestnut with a slice of the bacon and secure with a wooden pick. Pour the vegetable oil into a heavy pot or a deep fryer to about 3 inches deep and heat. Deep fry the water chestnuts for 4 to minutes or until the bacon is brown and crisp. Drain the bacon on a paper towel. Cool the water chestnuts and serve with the mustard sauce. The appetizer will serve eight guests. A sure winner!

Pesto Cheese Cake

½ cup crushed cheddar
  sesame cracker
Two 8-ounce packages
  cream cheese
2 eggs
4 tablespoons pesto
½ teaspoon salt
½ teaspoon cracked pepper
1 clove garlic
½ cup sour cream

¼ cup Parmesan cheese
Dash of salt
¼ teaspoon white pepper
½ cup sun-dried
  tomatoes
5 fresh basil leaves
Blanched broccoli florets,
  zucchini and
  cherry tomatoes

Line a coated 6-inch spring form pan with the cracker crumbs. Combine the cream cheese, eggs, pesto, ½ teaspoon salt, cracked pepper and garlic. Place the mixture on top of the cracker crumbs. Bake at 350 degrees for 30 to 40 minutes. Cool for 1 hour. Combine the sour cream, Parmesan cheese, dash of salt and white pepper. Place the mixture on top of the cream cheese mixture. Place the sun-dried tomatoes on top. Bake at 350 degrees for 10 minutes. Remove from the oven and chill for 3 hours. Remove the side of the pan and chill overnight. Decorate the top with the basil leaves and place the blanched vegetables down the sides. Serve with cheddar or your favorite crackers.

Refrigerator Rolls

1½ cups milk
¾ cup sugar
1½ teaspoons salt
2 eggs, beaten
1 cup oil

6 cups all-purpose flour
Two ¼-ounce packages
   active dry yeast
½ cup warm water
½ cup melted butter

These rolls will bring joy to all who love hot breads. They were Waylon's favorite. Be sure to make plenty, as each guest will eat several.

Scald the milk until a skim forms on the top. Add the sugar, salt, eggs and oil and stir well. Slowly add 3 cups of the flour. Pour the yeast in the water and allow to stand for 5 minutes. Add the yeast to the flour mixture. Cover and place in a warm oven for 1 hour. Remove from the oven and stir in the remaining 3 cups of flour. Refrigerate for 1 hour to 2 days. Roll the dough out on a floured board. Cut the dough into small circles. Dip each roll in the melted butter and fold each roll in half. Secure the roll by pressing lightly in the middle with your finger. Place the rolls on a baking sheet and lightly cover. Allow the rolls to rise for at least 4 hours. Bake at 400 degrees for 12 to 15 minutes or until lightly browned.

Connie Smith's Strawberry Cake

18¼-ounce box
   supreme white cake mix
3-ounce package
   strawberry gelatin
¾ cup oil
4 eggs, at room temperature
¼ cup water
½ cup butter

5 ounces
   frozen strawberries,
   thawed or 1 cup fresh
5 ounces
   frozen strawberries,
   thawed or 1 cup fresh
1-pound box
   powdered sugar

Combine the cake mix, gelatin and oil. Add the eggs, one at a time, alternating with the water. Add 5 ounces of the strawberries and beat with an electric mixer at medium speed for 3 minutes. Pour the mixture into three coated and floured 8-inch round cake pans. Bake at 325 degrees for 25 to 30 minutes. Test for doneness with a wooden pick. Remove from the oven and allow the cake to cool in the pans for 10 minutes before turning the layers onto a cooling rack.

Process the remaining 5 ounces of the strawberries in a blender container until smooth. Combine the butter, sugar and strawberries for the icing. Chill for 30 minutes. Frost the cake generously between the layers, on the top and sides.

Moon's Chocolate (Texas Sheet) Cake

1 stick butter or margarine
¼ cup shortening
4 tablespoons cocoa
1 cup water
2 cups sugar
2 cups flour
½ cup buttermilk
½ teaspoon salt
1 tablespoon cinnamon
2 eggs

1 teaspoon vanilla extract
1 tablespoon soda
1 stick butter
    or margarine
6 tablespoons milk
4 tablespoons cocoa
1 pound powdered sugar
1 cup chopped pecans
1 teaspoon vanilla extract

Combine the 1 stick of butter, shortening, 4 tablespoons of cocoa and water in a saucepan. Bring to a boil and pour over the sugar and flour in a bowl. Add the buttermilk, salt, cinnamon, eggs, 1 teaspoon vanilla extract and soda and beat well with an electric mixer. Pour the batter into a coated and floured 10x15-inch baking pan and bake at 400 degrees for 40 minutes.

Combine the 1 stick of butter, milk and the 4 tablespoons cocoa in a saucepan and bring to a boil. Beat in the powdered sugar with an electric mixer. Add the pecans and the 1 teaspoon vanilla extract and beat well. Frost the cake while warm.

Ralph Mooney is a legend in the country music field. He played on records cut by the greats. Buck Owens and Merle Haggard are only two of the many artists who depended on his style with the steel guitar. He traveled with us almost as long as we were together. Mrs. Mooney was loved by all who knew her. They're an award-winning pair! The recipes she shared with me have won me accolades at local bake sales.

Groom's Chocolate Cake

This was the groom's cake we made for Bill and Mandy Robinson's wedding. Bill was Waylon's agent from Los Angeles. They were married at Southern Comfort.

¾ cup butter
2 cups sugar
5 eggs
1 teaspoon soda
1 cup buttermilk
2 cups cake flour
3 squares unsweetened chocolate, melted
2 teaspoons vanilla extract
¼ teaspoon salt
1 cup cream
¾ cup sugar
1 cup chopped muscat raisins

1 teaspoon vanilla extract
1 cup chopped pecans
12-ounce package semisweet chocolate morsels
½ cup butter
1 cup sour cream
2 teaspoons vanilla extract
¼ teaspoon salt
6 cups powdered sugar, sifted

Cream the ¾ cup of butter until fluffy, adding the 2 cups of sugar slowly. Add the eggs, one at a time, beating well after each addition. Add the soda to the buttermilk. Add the flour and buttermilk, alternately, to the mixture. Pour in the chocolate, 2 teaspoons vanilla extract and ¼ teaspoon salt and mix well. Coat and flour four 8-inch round cake pans. Bake at 325 degrees for 25 to 30 minutes until a wooden pick comes out clean. Cool on racks until ready to assemble.

Pour the cream into a saucepan. Add the ¾ cup of the sugar and stir until the sugar is dissolved. Add the raisins and cook until thick. Cool and stir in the 1 teaspoon of the vanilla extract and pecans.

Melt the chocolate morsels and ½ cup of the butter in a saucepan over a low heat. Remove the saucepan from the heat and add the sour cream, 2 teaspoons vanilla extract and ¼ teaspoon salt and blend well. Add the powdered sugar, gradually, until the frosting is consistency for spreading.

Place the first cake layer on your loveliest cake plate. Pour ⅓ of the raisin filling on top of the first cake layer. Add the second cake layer and ⅓ of the filling. Add the third cake layer and the remaining filling. Place the last cake layer on the top. Spread a generous amount of the frosting on the top and sides of the cake.

Margie Veach's Decadent Fudge Cake

When Waylon was a boy, Margie Veach was his favorite baker. She grew up in England when sugar was scarce. Margie would call the children in from playing after baking their favorite chocolate cake, still warm from the oven.

1 cup butter softened
1½ cups sugar
4 eggs
1 cup buttermilk
½ teaspoon baking soda
2½ cups all-purpose flour
Two 4-ounce bars sweet
 baking chocolate,
 melted and cooled
1 cup chocolate syrup

2 teaspoons vanilla
 extract
1 cup semisweet
 chocolate mini-morsels
4 ounces white chocolate
 Bark or chips
2 tablespoons shortening
½ cup semisweet
 chocolate mini-morsels
2 teaspoons shortening
Chocolate and white
 chocolate leaves

Cream the butter in a large bowl. Add the sugar, gradually, beating with an electric mixer at medium speed. Add the eggs, one at a time, beating well after each addition.

Combine the buttermilk and baking soda, stirring well. Add the buttermilk mixture to the creamed mixture alternately with the flour, beginning and ending with the flour. Add the bars of chocolate, chocolate syrup and vanilla extract and mix well. Stir in the 1 cup of chocolate mini-morsels.

Pour the batter into a heavily coated and floured 10-inch bundt pan. Bake at 300 degrees for 1 hour and 20 minutes or until a wooden pick inserted in the center comes out clean. Invert the cake immediately onto a serving plate and allow to cool completely.

Combine the white chocolate and the 2 tablespoons of shortening in the top of a double boiler; bring the water to a boil. Reduce the heat to low

and cook until the white chocolate is melted and smooth. Remove from the heat. Drizzle the white chocolate mixture over the cooled cake. Melt the ½ cup of chocolate mini-morsels and the 2 teaspoons of shortening in a small saucepan over low heat, stirring until smooth. Remove from the heat and allow to cool. Drizzle the chocolate over the white chocolate. Garnish with the chocolate and white chocolate leaves, if desired. Makes one 10-inch cake.

Tammy Wynette's Banana Pudding

12-ounce box vanilla wafers	6 cups milk
1 cup self-rising flour	1 teaspoon vanilla extract
2 cups sugar	6 bananas, sliced
6 eggs, separated	½ cup sugar

Crumble the vanilla wafers and cover the bottom of a 9x13-inch glass baking dish to a 1 inch thickness. Set the dish aside.

Combine the flour and the 2 cups of sugar in the top of a double boiler and mix thoroughly. Add the egg yolks and mix well. Gradually add the milk and blend until smooth. Add the vanilla extract and cook at a medium heat until thickened, stirring continuously. Allow the mixture to cool to room temperature. Pour the mixture over the wafer crumbs and top evenly with the sliced bananas.

Beat the egg whites in a mixing bowl with an electric mixer. Gradually add the ½ cup of sugar and beat until the egg whites are stiff. Spread the meringue over the bananas and bake at 350 degrees for 8 to 10 minutes.

Serves 8

Tammy was famous far and wide for her banana pudding.

Note: You can substitute 7 tablespoons of artificial sweetener to make this lower in calories.

Texas Sky Scraper

Your guests will be delighted, however, the next day their scales may tell on them.

1 stick butter
1 cup flour
1 cup pecan chips
8 ounces cream cheese
1 cup whipped topping
1 cup powdered sugar

6-ounce package
  fudge pudding mix
1 cup whipping cream
1½ cups half-and-half
Whipped topping
1.55 ounce
  chocolate candy bar,
  grated

Combine the butter, flour and pecan chips. Press the mixture into a 9x13-inch glass baking dish. Bake at 350 degrees for 15 minutes. Allow to cool.

Combine the cream cheese, 1 cup whipped topping and sugar in a mixing bowl and beat with an electric mixer. Spread the cream cheese mixture over the cooled crust.

Prepare the fudge pudding mix according to the package directions; set aside to cool. Combine the pudding, whipping cream and half-and-half and mix well. Spread the chocolate mixture over the cream cheese mixture. Top with the whipped topping and the grated chocolate candy bar.

Serves 10

Mixed Curried Fruit

16-ounce can pears,
  drained
10-ounce can pineapple chunks,
  drained
16-ounce can peaches,
  drained

8-ounce can apricots,
  drained
8-ounce can cherries,
  drained
½ cup butter, melted
1 cup brown sugar
2 to 3 teaspoons
  curry powder

Combine the pears, pineapple, peaches, apricots and cherries and toss. Place the fruit in a 9x13-inch buttered baking dish. Combine the butter, brown sugar and curry powder. Pour the butter mixture over the fruit. Bake at 325 degrees for 30 to 40 minutes or until the fruit is hot and bubbly.

Serve from the dish or it is especially pretty from a fruit compote.

Serves 8 to 10

Marie's Chili

Toppings that may be added are grated cheese, chopped onion or chopped jalapeños. This is the best chili we've ever eaten!

1 pound spaghetti
1 pound dry pinto beans
1 tablespoon butter
2 pounds ground round
2 onions, finely chopped
2 cloves garlic, minced
1 to 2 tablespoons
   chili powder

½ teaspoon garlic salt
1 teaspoon salt
½ teaspoon pepper
1 tablespoon sugar
1 quart tomato juice
10¾-ounce can
   tomato soup
Parmesan cheese

Break the spaghetti into 3 pieces and cook according to the package directions to the al dente stage. Drain the spaghetti and set aside.

Soak the beans overnight or boil them for 3 to 5 minutes and remove from the heat and allow the beans to soak for 1 to 2 hours. Cook the pinto beans according to the package directions.

Heat the butter in a large skillet. Add the ground round, onions and garlic ; brown. Add the chili powder, garlic salt, salt, pepper and sugar while the meat is browning. Add the meat mixture, tomato juice and tomato soup to the undrained, cooked pinto beans. Simmer for 1 hour and stir in the spaghetti. Serve and sprinkle with the Parmesan cheese.

Serves 8 to 10

Paella

4 pounds chicken,
   cut into strips
2½ pounds Italian sausage
1 cup chopped onion
3 bell peppers, chopped
16-ounce can artichokes
3 cloves garlic, minced

4 cups rice
2 cups water or
   chicken broth
Pinch of saffron
5 bay leaves
Parsley, chopped
Tomato, chopped

Sauté the chicken and sausage in a skillet until brown. Add the onion, pepper, artichokes and garlic; sauté lightly. Add the rice and stir for 3 minutes. Add the water, saffron and bay leaves. Reduce the heat and cover after the mixture begins to boil. Cook for 20 to 25 minutes. Garnish with the parsley and tomato.

Filet Mignon à la Sherry

2 pounds filet mignon	1½ cups
Seasoned flour	chicken broth
2 tablespoons butter	1½ cups red wine
6 slices bacon	3 tablespoons
1 pound	cornstarch
sliced mushrooms	3 ounces water

Dredge the filet in the seasoned flour. Brown the filet in the butter in a skillet for 2 to 4 minutes on each side. Add the bacon and mushrooms and cook for 5 minutes. Remove the bacon slices. Add the chicken broth and wine and cook for 4 minutes (rare) to 10 minutes (well-done). Remove the meat and combine the cornstarch and water. Add the cornstarch mixture to the skillet and cook until slightly thickened to make the sauce. Pour the sauce in the center of a plate and place the meat on top. This is an exceptional recipe for company!

Beef Tenderloin

This is one of the easiest and most convenient ways to serve 8 to 10 people at a dinner party.

4 to 5 pound whole tenderloin	Garlic salt
Garlic powder	Freshly ground pepper
Lemon pepper	½ cup butter

Trim the excess fat from the tenderloin. Remove the thin bluish lining underneath the fat with a sharp knife. Sprinkle the tenderloin generously with the garlic powder, lemon pepper garlic salt and pepper. Rub the seasonings into the meat. Melt ¼ cup of the butter in a large skillet. Place the meat in the skillet and sear on all sides until brown. Place the meat in a coated roasting pan. Spread the remaining ¼ cup butter over the top of the meat. Bake at 400 degrees for 30 minutes (rare) to 45 minutes (medium). An internal temperature of 130 degrees is rare; 150 degrees is medium; and 160 degrees is well-done. I do not recommend well-done. We like ours medium to medium-well. You can estimate 8 ounces of meat per person before cooking. This will give each person about a 6-ounce portion after cooking. Serve with the Bordelaise Sauce.

Bordelaise Sauce

4 tablespoons butter
4 tablespoons minced celery
4 tablespoons minced carrots
¾ cup fresh mushrooms, sliced and sautéed
4 minced shallots
3 tablespoons minced parsley
¾ cup dry red wine

2¼ cups beef stock
1 teaspoon black pepper
1 teaspoon salt
1 teaspoon sugar
1 teaspoon whole thyme
½ teaspoon crushed coriander seed

Melt the butter in a saucepan. Sauté the celery, carrots, mushrooms, shallots and parsley for 5 minutes. Add the wine and simmer until the wine is reduced by half. Add the beef stock, pepper, salt, sugar, thyme and coriander. Simmer for 15 minutes. Thicken slightly if desired. Refrigerate up to 1 week.

Makes about 1 quart

Mesquite-Grilled T-Bones

The season was winter. Waylon was out on the road traveling and the day before we had received a big drum grill, along with a fresh supply of mesquite wood, from Arizona. Our good friend Bob Sikora had struck again.

The snow was four or five inches d veep and the moon was high. Our decorator, Bill Hamilton, was coming over to go over the plans for the guest room he'd prepared overnight (with the help of a marvelous crew) to receive our friend, James Garner, the next day. We had some T-bones in the fridge and I asked Bill if he'd stay to eat a bite. I put on my mink coat and French snow boots and stoked up the new grill. Mesquite catches on quickly, and before long, it seemed like Arizona in Tennessee. The steaks were done almost instantly. I doused the flame with a cup of water, then poured melted butter over the steaks, a method that really smokes the flavor into the meat. A salad, hot French bread and a glass of wine accompanied a night I'll never forget.

Baked Salmon Fillet with Beurre Blanc Sauce

3 tablespoons
   finely-chopped shallots
Six 6 to 8-ounce salmon fillets
1 cup white wine

Salt and
   white pepper to taste
3 tablespoons butter

Sprinkle the shallots on the bottom of a coated 9x13-inch baking dish. Place the dish in a 375 degree oven for 5 minutes. Remove the dish and place the salmon fillets on the top of the shallots. Sprinkle with the wine, salt and pepper. Rub the butter over the fillets using a piece of parchment paper. Place the parchment paper on top of the salmon. Return the dish to the oven and bake for 12 to 15 minutes. Use a fork to test for doneness. Remove the salmon from the pan and transfer to a serving plate. Pour the Beurre Blanc sauce over and around the salmon.

Serves 6

Buerre Blanc

6 shallots, peeled and minced
½ cup tarragon
   or white wine vinegar

½ pound unsalted butter
Salt and pepper to taste

Simmer the shallots in the vinegar in a saucepan for 10 minutes. Remove from the heat and cool slightly. Strain the shallots.

Whisk the butter, 1 tablespoon at a time, into the vinegar until smooth. Season with the salt and pepper. The mixture should have the same consistency as thin mayonnaise. Use immediately or keep warm. Do not reheat or the butter will melt and the mixture will separate.

Seafood Dijon

2 cups butter
2 teaspoons salt
4 tablespoons lemon juice
12 green onions with tops
½ teaspoon thyme
6 cups cubed bread
½ cup parsley
12 tablespoons
   beef bouillon

½ teaspoon
   Tabasco sauce
1 teaspoon dried chives
½ teaspoon tarragon
3 cups shrimp, lobster,
   crab meat
   or combination

Combine 1 cup butter, 1 teaspoon salt, 2 tablespoons lemon juice, 6 green onions, ¼ teaspoon thyme, 3 cups cubed bread, ¼ cup parsley, 6 tablespoons beef bouillon, ¼ teaspoon Tabasco sauce, ½ teaspoon chives and ¼ teaspoon tarragon in a food processor. Process until blended. Spread the mixture on the bottom of a 9x13-inch baking dish. Sauté the shrimp lightly in butter in a skillet. Select 4 to 5 lobster tails and steam until done. Cut the lobster tails into bite-size chunks. Pick over the crab meat to remove any shell. Place the seafood on top of the mixture. Waylon preferred lobster.

Place the remaining ingredients in a food processor and process until blended. Cover the seafood with the mixture. Bake at 350 degrees for 25 minutes or until bubbly and hot.

Sweet Oven–Baked Ham

18 to 20 pound
  sugar-cured ham
  with the bone in
	Chili powder
	Black pepper
	1½ cups water

Trim the skin and a small amount of the excess fat from of the ham. Rub generous amounts of the chili powder and black pepper over the ham. Pour the water in the bottom of a broiler pan. Do not let the water dry out at anytime during the cooking process. Cook at 500 degrees for 15 minutes. Reduce the heat to 375 degrees and cook allowing 25 minutes per pound of ham. The ham is done when the shank bone at this high heat dries out and it takes on a sweetness and a tenderness. It almost tastes like country ham, instead of sugar-cured ham.

We normally cook our hams slowly but we discovered this method and though it was so tender and sweet that we have been oven-cooking our holiday hams this way ever since.

Glaze

2 cups brown sugar ½ cup pineapple juice	1 tablespoon mustard 1 stick melted butter

Combine the brown sugar, pineapple juice, mustard and butter; mix well. Pour the glaze over the ham. Allow the ham to cool.

Veal Marsala

1½ pounds sliced veal
⅓ cup all-purpose flour
1 teaspoon salt
1 teaspoon pepper
1 tablespoon chopped parsley
4 tablespoons butter
3 tablespoons olive oil

½ pound
  sliced mushrooms,
  seasoned and sautéed
½ cup marsala
  or dry sherry
¼ cup chicken broth

Pound the veal slices on pieces of waxed paper until the veal is thin. Combine the flour, salt, pepper and parsley in a piepan distributing the seasonings evenly. Dredge the veal in the flour mixture.

Heat the butter and olive oil in a large skillet. Add the meat when the butter bubbles and begins to brown. Sauté the meat until golden on both sides. Place the sautéed mushrooms on the meat. Add the marsala and allow to bubble. Turn the meat. Cover the skillet and lower the heat and allow to simmer. Uncover and cook to form a thick gravy. Add the chicken broth if dry. Serve immediately.

Serves 4 to 6

Pasta Primavera with Seafood and Basil Cream

The pasta may be prepared up to 3 days ahead and the vegetable may be prepared up to 2 days ahead.

1 pound Italian fettuccini, broken into 2-inch pieces
1 tablespoon white wine
3 tablespoons light olive oil
½ tablespoon wine vinegar
Salt and freshly-ground pepper

Drop the pasta into 8 quarts of boiling, salted water. Boil rapidly until the pasta is tender but still firm to the bite. Drain the pasta, rinse with cold water and drain again. Place the pasta in a large bowl. Add the wine, oil and vinegar and toss lightly. Season to taste with the salt and pepper; toss again. Cover and chill.

16 very thin asparagus spears trimmed, cut into 1½-inch lengths
2 to 3 cups broccoli florets, cut in to bite-size pieces
2 to 3 cups fresh peas or tiny frozen peas, defrosted
8 green onions
1 pint small cherry tomatoes
1 pound fresh young spinach

Steam the asparagus, broccoli and peas until crisp-tender; do not overcook. Rinse the vegetables in cold water to stop the cooking process. Store the vegetable separately in resealable plastic bags in the refrigerator. Mince the green onions and halve the tomatoes. Place the onions and tomatoes in a small bowl and chill. Rinse the spinach leaves; wrap in plastic wrap and chill.

3 pounds uncooked large shrimp
1 pound cooked crab meat
3 tablespoons olive oil
½ tablespoon
   Spanish sherry wine vinegar

1 tablespoons
   white wine vinegar
1 clove garlic, minced
Salt and
   freshly-ground pepper

Poach the shrimp in their shells for 2 minutes or until they are pink and firm but not rubbery. Rinse the shrimp with cold water. Shell and devein; cut the shrimp in half. Place the shrimp and crab meat in a large bowl. Add the oil, vinegars and garlic. Season to taste with the salt and pepper; toss gently and chill.

Basil Cream

⅓ cup white wine vinegar
2 tablespoons Dijon mustard
½ cup fresh basil
2 large cloves garlic
⅓ cup vegetable oil

½ cup sour cream
½ cup whipping cream
3 tablespoons
   minced fresh parsley
   Salt and pepper

Combine the vinegar, mustard, basil and garlic in a food processor and mix until almost smooth. Drizzle in the oil while the processor is running. Add the sour cream, whipping cream and parsley and purée until smooth. Season to taste with the salt and pepper. Chill until ready to serve. Stir several times and pour into a serving bowl. Add more sour cream if thickening is needed.

Arrange the spinach leaves around the outer edge of a large serving platter. Toss the pasta, vegetables and green onion mixture gently.

Arrange the mixture in the center of the platter using the spinach leaves as a border. Make a well in the center of the pasta. Mound the seafood in center of pasta. Drizzle with the Basil Cream and serve the remaining Basil Cream in a bowl on the side.

Wild Rice Pilaf

1 cup wild rice
1 onion, chopped
¼ pound fresh mushrooms
3 celery stalks, chopped
¼ cup chopped green pepper
½ red pepper, chopped
2 carrots, diced

3 tablespoons butter
3 cups chicken broth,
  heated
½ cup sliced almonds
½ teaspoon thyme
Salt and pepper to taste

Wash the wild rice in cold water and drain. Lightly sauté the onion, mushrooms, celery, peppers, carrots and wild rice in 2 tablespoons of the butter. Brown the almonds in the remaining 1 tablespoon butter. Pour the vegetables into a coated 3-quart baking dish. Stir in the chicken broth. Add the almonds, thyme, salt and pepper and mix well. Bake at 325 degrees for 1½ hours or until the liquid is absorbed and the rice grains are puffed open.

Serves 6

Grilled Salmon Salad

2 large bunches romaine lettuce
1 red bell pepper
1 English cucumber
5 green onions
1 large red onion,
   sliced and separated
2 tomatoes, chopped

Four 8-ounce
   salmon fillets
Juice of lemon and lime
2 teaspoons olive oil
Paul Prudhomme's
   Seafood Magic
1 cup honey mustard
   dressing

Chop the lettuce, pepper, cucumber and green onions. Toss the vegetables in a bowl and place the red onion and tomatoes on top.

Wash the salmon fillets and pat dry with a paper towel. Squeeze the lemon and lime juice on the salmon fillets. Lightly brush each fillet with the oil and coat each side with the Seafood Magic. Grill the salmon for 5 minutes per side or until the salmon flakes easily. Cut the fillets into bite-size chunks.

Place the salad greens on four large dinner plates. Place the grilled salmon chunks on top of the salad. Drizzle the honey mustard dressing over the top of the salad and salmon. Grind fresh black pepper over the salad.

Serves 4

Hot Chicken Salad

4 cups cooked, cubed chicken
4 tablespoons lemon juice
¾ cup mayonnaise
2 cups chopped celery
2 hard-boiled eggs, sliced
¾ cup cream of chicken soup
1 large onion, finely chopped

2 teaspoons
   chopped pimento
1 cup grated
   Cheddar cheese
⅔ cup toasted
   almond slivers
1½ cups
   crushed potato chips

Combine the chicken, lemon juice, mayonnaise, celery, eggs, soup, onion and pimento in a large bowl; mix well. Cover and chill overnight. Place the mixture in a baking dish and top with the cheese, almonds and potato chips. Bake at 400 degrees for 20 to 25 minutes.

Serves 8

Dill Sauce

1 clove elephant garlic
1 tablespoon Dijon mustard
2 tablespoons
   white wine vinegar
1 egg yolk
1½ cups fresh chopped dill

½ cup olive oil
¼ cup whipping cream
Salt and freshly
   ground pepper to taste
Juice of ½ lemon

Combine the garlic, mustard, vinegar, egg yolk and dill in a blender container or food processor and process until smooth. Pour a thin stream of

the olive oil into the blender container while processing. Process until the mixture begins to thicken. Continue processing and add the cream. Turn the blender off when the cream is mixed. Stir in the salt and lemon juice. Add a few drops of cream if the sauce is too thick.

Artichokes Smothered with Tomatoes and Herbs

4 artichokes
4 shallots, finely minced
4 small onions, chopped
4 tablespoons olive oil
4 tablespoons chopped parsley

8 medium tomatoes, peeled
Freshly-ground pepper
1 teaspoon salt

Cut the stem and pointed top from the artichokes. Trim the prickly points from the leaves with scissors. Soak the artichokes in a bowl of water and lemon juice for 30 minutes to soften and prevents discoloration. Remove the artichokes and pry apart the center of the artichokes. Scoop out the hairy core with a sharp teaspoon, being careful not to tear off outer leaves. This takes a little practice, but artichokes are very resilient and will take a lot of punishment. Stand the artichokes upright in a deep baking dish.

Combine the shallots, onions, olive oil, parsley, tomatoes, pepper and salt. Spoon a small amount of the mixture into the center cavity of each artichoke. Sprinkle the remaining mixture over the tops and between the outer leaves. Add enough water to cover the bottom third of the artichokes. Bring to a boil and reduce heat to simmer. Cover and cook for 30 to 45 minutes or until the artichokes are tender. Serve hot, warm or at room temperature.

Serves 4

Braised Brussels Sprouts

1 pound brussels sprouts
4 tablespoons butter

Salt and pepper to taste

Wash and trim the brussels sprouts. Cook the brussels sprouts in a large kettle of boiling, salted water for 5 minutes . Drain the brussels sprouts and place them in a heavy baking dish. Top with the butter, salt and pepper. Cover the sprouts with a piece of buttered brown or parchment paper. Place the cover on the dish. Bake at 350 degrees for 20 to 30 minutes or until the brussels sprouts are tender.

Oven-Baked Asparagus

6 to 8 stalks asparagus per person
Salt
Pepper

Lemon juice
Butter
Parmesan cheese

Wash the asparagus stalks; break or cut the asparagus stalks where the tender part ends and the tough, woodsy part of the stem begins. Cut the asparagus with a knife for uniformity. Place the asparagus in aluminum foil and sprinkle with the salt, pepper and lemon juice. Dot with the butter. Bake at 325 degrees for 20 to 30 minutes, depending on how tender you like the asparagus; twenty minutes for crisp, thirty minutes for soft, but not over done. Sprinkle with the Parmesan cheese and serve.

Three-Bean Baked Beans

1 medium onion, chopped
4 slices bacon,
    cut into bite-size pieces
32-ounce can pork and beans,
    pork removed
16-ounce can lima beans,
    drained
16-ounce can kidney beans,
    drained

½ cup brown sugar
⅓ cup ketchup
2 teaspoons
    Worcestershire sauce
½ pound Velveeta
    cheese, cut up
½ cup Parmesan cheese

Brown the onion and bacon lightly in a large skillet. Stir in the pork and beans, lima beans, kidney beans, brown sugar and ketchup. Add the Worcestershire sauce and Velveeta cheese. Cook until the cheese melts, stirring until blended. Pour the beans into a coated 9x13-inch baking dish. Sprinkle with the Parmesan cheese. Bake at 325 degrees for 30 minutes.

Serves 12

Waylon's Spinach Casserole

Four 10-ounce packages
  frozen chopped spinach
½ pound fresh mushrooms,
  sliced
¾ cup butter
½ cup mayonnaise
1 cup sour cream

1 cup freshly grated
  Romano cheese
8½-ounce can artichokes,
  drained and quartered
2 tomatoes, sliced thin
⅔ cup fresh bread
  crumbs

Cook the spinach according to the package directions and drain. Sauté the mushrooms in ¼ cup of the butter. Combine the mayonnaise, sour cream, and ⅔ cup of the Romano cheese; stir in the spinach, mushrooms and artichokes. Pour the mixture into a coated 9x13-inch baking dish. Arrange the tomatoes on top. Top the casserole with the bacon. Melt the remaining ½ cup of butter, stir in the bread crumbs and the remaining ⅓ cup of Romano cheese. Sprinkle the crumb mixture over the top of the casserole. Bake at 350 degrees for 30 minutes.

This may be made a day ahead, covered and chilled, then baked for approximately 40 minutes when ready to serve.

Scalloped Potatoes

8 large baking potatoes
Salt and pepper to taste
Paprika
2 tablespoons flour
½ cup butter
8 ounces mushrooms, sliced
1 green pepper, chopped

1 red pepper,
    chopped
1 large onion,
    chopped
8 ounces grated
    Colby cheese
1½ cups cream

Boil the potatoes in their jackets for 15 minutes or until they are half done. Test them with a fork, the outside should be tender and the middle still slightly hard. Remove the potatoes and allow them to cool slightly, just enough for handling. Peel and slice the potatoes into ¼-inch slices. Place ⅓ of the potatoes on the bottom of a coated 9x13-inch baking dish. Sprinkle the potatoes with the salt, pepper, paprika, 1 tablespoon of the flour and 2 tablespoons of the butter. Layer ½ of the mushrooms, peppers and onion. Sprinkle ⅓ of the cheese over the top. Layer ⅓ of the potatoes and sprinkle with the salt, pepper, paprika, 1 tablespoon of the flour and 2 tablespoons of the butter. Place the remaining mushrooms, onion and peppers on top. Sprinkle ⅓ of the cheese on top. Place the remaining potatoes on the top. Sprinkle with the salt, pepper and paprika and dot with 4 tablespoons of the butter. Layer the remaining cheese on the top and pour the cream over the top. Cover and bake at 300 degrees for 1 hour.

Serves 8 to 10

Note: This recipe can be made low-fat by omitting the butter, doubling the flour, using light cheese and substituting the cream with evaporated skim milk.

Maureen preparing low fat foods.

Grilled Salmon, page 133,
Tomato Linguini, page 138,
and a steamed
vegatable medley.

Low Fat Years

Maureen Raffety is qualified to help others lose weight because she has experienced the agony of being overweight. She has proven that others can benefit from her personal experiences.

During 1944, seeing a pediatrician for nutritional advice was a fairly new thing. Maureen's pediatrician was fond of suggesting menus for babies that were very rich and high in fat. Maureen's mother paid strict attention to the doctor's guidelines, and dreamed up delightful meals for her, making sure she ate heartily.

Many doctors today believe that fat cells that are developed as a baby will lead to being overweight in the future. By the age of 16 Maureen had lost her first 50 pounds. She would repeat this process many times throughout her life, with hope that the weight would not return.

However, her fight against weight still continues today. Even though she had been instrumental in changing Waylon's diet, she sought the help of a nutritionist to change hers.

During this sixteen month period she lost 191 pounds by adhering faithfully to a 1200 calorie, 20 fat gram diet, and walking 5 miles a day. With the guidelines prescribed by the nutritionist, she was able to create wonderful menus for herself, and soon friends and family were asking her to design weight-loss plans for them.

Chutney Cheese Canapé

8-ounce package
   light cream cheese
¼ cup chutney
¼ teaspoon dry mustard
1 teaspoon curry powder

1 small pineapple,
   cut in half lengthwise
½ cup sliced,
   toasted almonds

Blend the cream cheese, chutney, mustard and curry powder in a food processor and mix well. Scoop out the inside of the pineapple and set aside. Fill half of the pineapple with the cream cheese mixture. Cover and chill until ready to serve. Sprinkle the cream cheese mixture with the almonds before serving.

Cut the pineapple into bite-size pieces. Serve the pineapple chunks and strawberries on wooden skewers, along with crackers.

The Low-Fat Years

As we've moved through the phases of our lives, we have learned to bend with the winds of change. Waylon's bypass surgery was the storm that turned the sails of Southern Comfort in the direction of "food for life."

Today we eat low fat, low sugar and low sodium foods. We've learned that healthy food provides high-energy fuel and may be prepared with style and beauty, sacrificing nothing.

Join us as we celebrate the joy of a table filled with food that is both good to eat and good for you.

NOTE: If you are serious about weight loss, you may spend 22 fat grams a day anyway you like and you will lose weight (along with exercise). Maureen tested men and women alike at this count and it remains the magic number.

Flavor Without Fat

I don't mean to brag, but I have to say that when people eat at Southern Comfort they never forget it. They even talk about it at other people's houses. We were amused when Robert Duvall ate at our house and obviously loved it, but told us about the meal June Carter Cash had prepared for

Skinny Dip

1 cup light mayonnaise
2 tablespoons Durkee sauce
1 tablespoon horseradish
1 teaspoon celery seed
½ teaspoon Worcestershire sauce
½ teaspoon garlic salt
1 teaspoon curry powder

1 teaspoon seasoned salt
½ teaspoon
    Beau Monde seasoning
Dash of pepper
¼ teaspoon sugar
Chopped parsley

Combine the mayonnaise, Durkee sauce, horseradish, celery seed, Worcestershire sauce and garlic salt in a bowl. Add the curry powder, seasoned salt, Beau Monde seasoning, pepper and sugar and mix well. Chill, covered, overnight. Garnish with the chopped parsley. Serve with fresh, raw vegetables.

Makes 1½ cups

him during a Nashville visit. He learned to play us one against the other until he had us competing.

But today when people talk about eating at Southern Comfort the food is a little different from the traditional Southern fare. We eat lots of vegetables, such as English cucumbers (less seedy), yellow tomatoes (less acidic), and sweet onions from Chile in the winter. Summertime always finds us happily gobbling small homegrown cucumbers, plump ripe red tomatoes, and juicy melons of all kinds (yellow meated watermelon was Waylon's favorite).

Our large fresh loaves of home-baked breads include rye, diet white and buttermilk. Our

meats are from organic sources and we eat a maximum of 6 ounces of meat per day. Spices come from all over the world and by trial and error we've found our favorite combinations.

Maureen developed low-fat versions of our favorite foods and introduced us to a wide variety of dishes from around the world while keeping the fat-gram count low. Here are some of the specialties from the healthy menus at Southern Comfort.

Tuna Pâte

8-ounce package
  light cream cheese, softened
1 cup chopped onion
1 tablespoon Worcestershire sauce
2 tablespoons chili sauce

2 tablespoons chopped,
  fresh parsley
½ teaspoon
  Tabasco sauce
Two 7-ounce cans
  white tuna in water,
  drained

Combine the cream cheese, onion, Worcestershire sauce, chili sauce, parsley and Tabasco sauce; stir well. Add the tuna and mix well. Chill for at least 3 hours before serving. Serve with assorted crackers.

Arrangement of the food is a big part of the beauty.

Ninety Minute Dinner Rolls

1 cup unsifted flour
2 tablespoons sugar
½ teaspoon salt
¼-ounce package active
   dry yeast

½ cup 2% milk
¼ cup water
2 tablespoons margarine

Combine ¾ cup of the flour, sugar, salt and yeast in a large bowl. Heat the milk, water and margarine in a saucepan to 120 to 130 degrees. Add the milk mixture to the dry ingredients gradually and beat for 2 minutes with an electric mixer. Add ¼ cup of the flour and beat on high for 2 minutes. Stir in enough additional flour to make a soft dough. Turn the dough onto a floured board and knead for 2 to 3 minutes. Divide the dough into 12 equal pieces and shape into balls. Place the balls into a coated 8-inch round pan. Allow to rise in a warm place. Bake at 375 degrees for 20 to 25 minutes. Serve warm.

Makes 12 rolls

Sour Cream Corn Bread

1 cup self-rising cornmeal
1 cup cream-style corn
2 eggs

1 cup light sour cream
⅓ cup canola oil

Combine the cornmeal, corn, eggs, sour cream and canola oil and beat well. Pour the batter into a cast-iron skillet that has been coated with vegetable spray. Bake at 425 degrees for 25 minutes or until golden brown.

Angel Hair Pasta Primavera

4 quarts chicken broth
16 ounces angel hair pasta
1 cup chopped carrots
1 red bell pepper, diced
1 green bell pepper, diced
2 cups julienned zucchini

¼ cup olive oil
4 chicken breasts,
    grilled and sliced
    into thin strips
½ cup Parmesan cheese
Salt and pepper to taste

Bring the chicken broth to a rapid boil in a large pot. Add the pasta to the boiling chicken broth and cook, uncovered, for 4 to 6 minutes or until the desired tenderness is reached. Stir the pasta occasionally; drain well and set aside.

Sauté the carrots, peppers and zucchini in the olive oil in a skillet until tender. Toss the vegetables and pasta. Add the grilled chicken and Parmesan cheese. Season with the salt and pepper.

Serves 4

Authentic Italian Mostaccioli

¼ cup olive oil
2 cloves garlic, crushed
1¼ teaspoons salt
¾ cup finely-chopped onion
3½ cups crushed tomatoes
Two 6-ounce cans tomato paste
1½ cups water
¼ teaspoon pepper
2 teaspoons sugar
¼ cup finely-chopped parsley
2 teaspoons grated lemon rind

2 bay leaves
½ teaspoon oregano
½ teaspoon basil
1 pound lean
   ground round
½ pound ground veal
16 ounces
   mostaccioli pasta
Parmesan cheese
Pepper to taste

Heat the olive oil in 7 a deep 4 ½ to 5-quart saucepan or Dutch oven. Add the garlic, salt and onion to the hot oil and sauté until the onion is tender. Add the tomatoes, tomato paste, water, pepper, sugar, parsley, lemon rind and bay leaves; mix well. Bring the mixture to a boil and turn the heat to low; simmer for 20 minutes. Add the oregano and basil the last 10 minutes. Brown the ground round and veal in a skillet until all the pink is gone. Add the cooked meat to the sauce and cover. Simmer for 2 hours. Check for moisture and add additional water if necessary. The sauce should be very thick, but not dry.

Prepare the mostaccioli according to the package directions. Place the mostaccioli on a hot platter and top with the sauce. Repeat layers if desired. Sprinkle each layer with the Parmesan cheese and pepper.

Serves 8 to 10

Chicken and Black Bean Enchiladas

¾ pound skinless,
   boneless chicken breasts
3 slices bacon
2 cloves garlic, minced
1½ cups picante sauce
16-ounce can black beans,
   drained
1 large red bell pepper,
   chopped
2 teaspoons ground cumin
¼ teaspoon salt

1 cup sliced
   green onions
Twelve 6 to 7-inch
   flour tortillas
1½ cups shredded
   light Monterey Jack
   cheese
Shredded lettuce
Chopped tomato
Light sour cream
Avocado slices

Cut the chicken into short, thin strips. Cook the bacon in a skillet until the bacon is crisp. Remove the bacon to a paper towels; crumble. Pour off all but 2 tablespoons of the bacon drippings. Cook the chicken and garlic in the drippings until the chicken is no longer pink. Stir in ½ cup of the picante sauce, beans, pepper, cumin and salt. Simmer for 7 to 8 minutes or until thickened, stirring occasionally. Stir in the green onions and bacon. Spoon a heaping ¼ cup of the bean mixture in the center of each tortilla; top with 1 tablespoon of the cheese. Roll the tortillas up and place the tortillas seam side down in a lightly coated 9x13-inch baking dish. Spoon the remaining 1 cup of picante sauce evenly over the enchiladas. Bake at 350 degrees for 15 minutes. Top with the lettuce, tomato, sour cream and avocados. Serve with additional picante sauce.

Serves 6

Stuffed Pepper Cups

4 to 6 green peppers
½ pound ground round
½ pound ground veal
½ cup chopped onion
¼ cup chopped green pepper
1 teaspoon garlic salt
½ teaspoon pepper
1 tablespoon soy sauce
2 tablespoons sugar
1 tablespoon picante sauce

6-ounce can
   diced tomatoes
8-ounce can
   tomato sauce
½ cup uncooked wild
   or long grain
   white rice
1 cup shredded
   light Velveeta cheese
½ cup ketchup

Cut the tops off of the peppers. Remove the seeds and membrane. Cook the cups and the tops in boiling water for 5 to 7 minutes. Drain and sprinkle the inside of the cups generously with salt and a pinch of sugar.

Cook the ground round and veal in a skillet until the meat is lightly browned. Add the onion, green pepper, garlic salt, pepper, soy sauce, sugar and picante sauce. Cook until the onion is tender and transparent. Add the tomatoes, tomato sauce and rice. Cover and simmer for 15 to 20 minutes or until the rice is tender. Add ¼ to ½ cup of water if too dry. Add ½ cup of the cheese, stirring until the cheese is melted.

Stuff the peppers with the meat mixture and place the tops back on. Sprinkle the remaining cheese over the tops. Drizzle the ketchup over the cheese. Stand the peppers upright in a baking dish. Cover and bake at 350 degrees for 25 minutes.

Serves 4 to 6

Southern Comfort Meat Loaf

¾ pound ground lean veal
¾ pound ground sirloin
2 eggs, beaten
8-ounce can tomato sauce
½ cup finely-chopped onion
¼ cup chopped green pepper
¼ cup chopped red pepper
1 tablespoon
   Worcestershire sauce

1 teaspoon salt
¼ teaspoon pepper
1 cup Ritz
   cracker crumbs
Dash of dried thyme
Dash of marjoram
½ cup ketchup
¼ cup dark corn syrup

Combine the veal, sirloin, eggs, tomato sauce, onion, peppers, Worcestershire sauce, salt, pepper, crumbs, thyme and marjoram; mix well. Pat the mixture into a loaf baking dish. Bake, uncovered, at 350 degrees for 1½ hours. Combine the ketchup and corn syrup. Spread the ketchup mixture evenly on top of the loaf the last thirty minutes of cooking.

Serves 6 to 8

Cajun Grilled Halibut

This recipe serves one, adjust the ingredients for the number served.

One 8-ounce halibut fillet
Lemon and lime juice

1 tablespoon olive oil
Paul Prudhomme's
    Seafood Magic

Wash the halibut and place the halibut on paper towels and pat dry. Squeeze the lemon and lime juice over both sides of the halibut. Brush both sides of the halibut with the olive oil. Sprinkle the Seafood Magic generously on both sides of the halibut. Place the halibut on a preheated grill. Grill for 3 to 5 minutes per side. Allow 5 minutes for each side per inch of the fish. Serve with lemon wedges.

Grilled Salmon

One 8 to 10-ounce
    salmon fillet per person
Lemon juice
Lime juice
Olive oil

Paul Prudhomme's
    Seafood Magic
Low-fat honey mustard
    dressing

Sprinkle each fillet generously with the lemon and lime juices. Brush each side lightly with the olive oil. Sprinkle the Seafood Magic generously on each side of the salmon. Pour the honey mustard dressing over the fillet and chill for 3 to 8 hours.

Grill over medium-hot coals for 3 to 5 minutes per side depending on the thickness of your fillet or until the salmon flakes easily.

This recipe is good for halibut, swordfish and bass.

Stuffed Pork Loin

2 green peppers
2 red peppers
6 to 7 pound pork loin
Freshly-ground pepper
2 tablespoons
   finely-diced shallots
3 cloves garlic

Minced parsley
Fresh herbs
1 tablespoon olive oil
1 tablespoon butter
1 cup white wine
1 quart chicken stock

Place the peppers on a baking sheet and char evenly under the broiler, turning and watching carefully. Place the charred peppers in a resealable plastic bag for 15 to 30 minutes. Remove and rub the blackened skin off of the peppers.

Lay the pork loin, fat side down, on a cutting board. Cut into the meat at an angle without actually cutting through. Fold the meat back and gently pound out until almost double in size. Season the loin with the pepper. Cut the roasted peppers into 2-inch strips and place the peppers onto the meat lengthwise. Place the shallots, garlic, parsley and herbs gently on the pork loin. Roll the meat and tie it with a string to hold it in place. Heat the olive oil and butter in a large skillet over a medium-high heat until lightly foaming. Place the pork loin, fat side down, in the oil and butter, turning gently until brown on all sides and both ends. Remove the pork loin to a roasting pan. Deglaze the skillet with the white wine. Add the chicken stock and bring to a boil. Pour the mixture over the pork loin. Cover the pork loin and cook at 350 degrees for 50 minutes. Uncover and cook for 40 minutes, basting every 10 to 15 minutes. Remove the pork loin from the oven and place on a platter to cool for 10 minutes.

Slice the pork loin into medium-thick slices and place on a warm serving platter. Reduce the pan juices by ½ and pour the juices over the meat before serving.

Serves 16

Chicken Schnitzel

6 boneless skinless breasts,
   flattened
12 ounces milk

Garlic salt
2 to 3 cups
   butter cracker crumbs

Soak the flattened chicken breasts in the milk for at least 2 hours in the refrigerator. Remove the chicken from the milk and lightly sprinkle with the garlic salt. Press the cracker crumbs into the chicken. Lay the chicken on waxed paper and chill until ready to fry. Heat a small amount of olive oil in a skillet. Dredge the chicken breasts a second time in the cracker crumbs. Fry until golden brown. Drain on paper towels.

Serves 6

Sauerkraut and New Potatoes

1 quart deli sauerkraut
Two 14½-ounce cans
   new potatoes, undrained

1 teaspoon dill seed

Rinse the sauerkraut. Combine the sauerkraut, potatoes and dill seed in a saucepan. Simmer for 2 hours. Add enough water as needed to make juice. Serve over Chicken Schnitzel. Place 1 to 2 of the chicken breasts in the middle of a serving plate. Pour 1 cup of the sauerkraut and potatoes on top of the chicken and add ¼ cup pickled red cabbage on the side for color. A salad and a nice rye dill bread goes well with it also.

Serves 4 to 6

Hawaiian Chicken Kabobs

6 thin chicken breast fillets
2 large purple or sweet onions
1 green bell pepper
1 red bell pepper
8 ounces fresh mushrooms
15-ounce can pineapple spears
Garlic salt
Lemon pepper

½ cup loosely-packed
   brown sugar
1 tablespoon
   Dijon mustard
2 tablespoons soy sauce
3 tablespoons olive oil
1 teaspoon salt
½ teaspoon black pepper

Cut the chicken into 1½-inch cubes. Quarter the onion and separate into pieces. Cut the green and red peppers into similar size pieces. Wash the mushrooms and remove the stems. Drain the pineapple, reserving the juice.

Fill 4 long skewers, alternating the chicken, vegetables and pineapple. Lay the skewers in a baking dish and season generously with the garlic salt and lemon pepper.

Combine the brown sugar, dijon mustard, soy sauce, olive oil, pineapple juice, salt and pepper. Pour the marinade over the kabobs and marinate for 4 to 24 hours in the refrigerator.

Grill the kabobs over a medium flame for 25 minutes, occasionally basting with the marinade.

Veal Scaloppini With Tomatoes

1½ pounds veal,
   pounded an
   cut into 1-inch squares
¾ cup all-purpose flour
1 tablespoon butter
1 tablespoon olive oil
½ pound mushrooms,
   thinly sliced
1 clove garlic, minced

2 tablespoons
   chopped fresh parsley
1 tablespoon
   chopped fresh basil
1 cup peeled, seeded and
   diced fresh tomatoes
½ cup marsala wine
2 tablespoons grated
   Parmesan cheese

Dredge the veal in the flour. Brown the veal in the butter and olive oil in a large skillet. Add the mushrooms and cook for 5 minutes. Add the garlic, parsley and basil; cook for 1 minute. Add the tomatoes and cook for 5 minutes. Stir in the wine. Pour the mixture into a baking dish. Sprinkle the Parmesan cheese on top and bake at 325 degrees for 45 minutes.

Serves 4

Tomato Linguini with Garlic Sauce

3 quarts water
12 ounces dried tomato
    linguini pasta
2 tablespoons olive oil
1 red bell pepper, diced
1 onion, chopped
1 clove garlic, chopped
2 tablespoons flour
15-ounce can chicken broth
1 tablespoon dried onion
1 teaspoon dried minced garlic

1 teaspoon oregano
¼ teaspoon
    red pepper flakes
1 teaspoon salt
1 tablespoon
    dried parsley
½ teaspoon black pepper
Bay leaf
½ cup freshly-grated
    Romano cheese,
    optional

Bring the water to a rapid boil in a large stockpot, add the pasta and cook until it reaches the al dente stage. Drain, rinse and redrain; set aside.

Heat the olive oil in a large skillet over a medium heat. Sauté the red pepper, onion and garlic until tender. Stir in the flour. Add the chicken broth, dried onion, minced garlic, oregano, red pepper flakes, salt, parsley, pepper and bay leaf. Cook until the mixture begins to thicken slightly. Add the drained pasta to the sauce and toss well until the pasta is hot. Add the grated cheese and serve.

Serves 6 as a side dish or 3 as a main dish

Big Cedar Oriental Crunchy Salad

2 tablespoons sesame seeds
½ cup slivered almonds
16-ounce bag shredded cabbage
3-ounce package oriental
  flavor ramen noodles, uncooked

4 chopped green onions
2 tablespoons sugar
½ cup oil
3 tablespoons
  wine vinegar

Toast the sesame seeds and almonds. Combine the cabbage, noodles, onions, sesame seeds and almonds in a bowl. Combine the sugar, oil, vinegar and ramen noodle seasoning packet. Pour the dressing over the cabbage mixture. Add shredded chicken if desired. This salad is best if it is not made in advance.

The Big Cedar Lodge outside Branson, Missouri served this on a trail ride and fishing expedition. It was a big hit with Waylon.

Grilled Chicken Salad

6 boneless, skinless
   chicken breasts
2 tablespoons olive oil
Paul Prudhomme's
   Poultry Magic
2 bunches Romaine lettuce
8 green onions, sliced thin
1 purple onion, sliced diagonally
1 cucumber, diced

2 tomatoes, diced
1 red bell pepper,
   cut into strips
Two 6.7-ounce boxes
   Uncle Ben's long grain
   & wild rice original
   5-minute recipe
1 cup low-fat
   honey mustard
   dressing

Baste the chicken breasts in the olive oil and sprinkle generously with the Poultry Magic. Chill for 2 to 8 hours. Discard the outer leaves of the lettuce. Chop or tear the lettuce into bite-size pieces. Add the green onions, purple onion, cucumber, tomatoes and pepper. Grill the chicken until done. Slice the chicken into thin long strips, approximately ¼-inch thick. Cook the rice according to the package directions.

Place the salad in a big circle on each plate leaving a small hole in the center. Place 1 cup of the rice in the hole. Place the chicken on top of each salad. Spoon the dressing over the entire salad. Sprinkle with freshly ground pepper and serve.

Serves 6

Hearty Cabbage Soup

1½ pounds ground round
1 onion, chopped
1 small head cabbage, chopped
3 cups water
2 chopped leeks
Three 14½-ounce cans
  chicken broth
1 bay leaf

1 teaspoon salt
2 tablespoons
  Worcestershire sauce
1 tablespoon sugar or
  1 pack sugar substitute
Two 6-ounce cans
  tomato paste

Brown the ground round and onion in a skillet. Combine the cabbage, water, leeks, chicken broth, bay leaf, salt, Worcestershire sauce and sugar in a saucepan. Bring the mixture to a boil; reduce the heat and simmer for 1 hour. Add the tomato paste and cook for 30 minutes.

Serves 6 to 8

Good for cold winter evenings.

Stir-Fry Bright Flower Shrimp

1 cup cubed yellow squash
1 cup sliced mushrooms
1 cup small broccoli florets
1 cup sliced zucchini
1 cup julienned red pepper
1 tablespoon olive oil
2 teaspoons soy sauce
4 garlic cloves, minced

1 teaspoon ginger root
¼ teaspoon crushed
 red pepper flakes
Two 14-ounce cans
 chicken broth
Cornstarch
1½ to 2 pounds shrimp
1 box basmati rice

Sauté the squash, mushrooms, broccoli, zucchini and pepper in the olive oil in a large skillet. Remove the skillet from the heat. Combine the soy sauce, garlic, ginger root, red pepper and chicken broth in a saucepan and simmer. Thicken the sauce to the desired consistency with the cornstarch. Stir fry the shrimp. Cook the rice according to the package directions. Combine the vegetables, rice, shrimp and sauce. Great dish for company.

Southwestern Bean and Chicken Soup

1 large onion, chopped
1 tablespoon olive oil
16-ounce can kidney beans,
    undrained
16-ounce can pinto beans,
    drained
Two 4-ounce cans
    chopped green chiles
16-ounce can corn, undrained
Three 14½-ounce cans
    chicken broth

1½ teaspoons
    ground cumin
2 tablespoons
    dried oregano
1 teaspoon garlic powder
⅛ teaspoon
    ground red pepper
4 grilled
    chicken breasts

Sauté the onion in the olive oil in a Dutch oven until the onion is transparent. Add the beans, chiles, corn, chicken broth, cumin, oregano, garlic powder and red pepper. Cover and bring to a boil. Reduce the heat and simmer for 30 minutes. Dice the cooled chicken and add it to the soup. Cook for 15 minutes.

Serves 6

Tomato Florentine Soup

1 large onion, chopped
1 clove garlic, minced
2 cups finely-diced celery
1 tablespoon olive oil
Two 14½-ounce
   cans diced tomatoes
Two 14½-ounce
   cans tomato wedges
Two 14½-ounce
   cans stewed tomatoes
Two 10¾-ounce
   cans tomato soup
8 cups chicken stock
   or canned chicken broth

2 tablespoons sugar
1½ teaspoons salt
1 tablespoon oregano
2 cups finely-chopped
   fresh spinach
8 ounces dry pasta shells
   or baby bow tie pasta
4 ounces shredded
   Parmesan cheese
1 teaspoon cream
¼ cup finely-chopped
   fresh parsley
Freshly-ground pepper

Sauté the onion, garlic and celery in the olive oil in a Dutch oven until the vegetables are tender. Add the diced tomatoes, tomato wedges, stewed tomatoes, tomato soup, chicken broth, sugar, salt and oregano; simmer for 2 hours. Add the spinach and cook for 10 minutes. Cook the pasta according to the package directions to the al dente stage; add the pasta to the vegetable mixture. Stir in the Parmesan cheese, cream, parsley and pepper. Serve immediately.

Serves 8 to 10

Vegetable Chowder

2 quarts low-sodium
  chicken broth
  or homemade stock
4 potatoes, diced
5 fresh tomatoes, diced
1 onion, diced
1 cup diced celery
1 cup shredded cabbage
1 cup small cauliflower florets
1 bay leaf
¼ cup finely-chopped
  fresh parsley
¼ teaspoon red pepper flakes
Dash of freshly-ground
  black pepper

2 tablespoons sugar
¼ teaspoon garlic powder
¼ teaspoon oregano
¼ teaspoon basil
¼ teaspoon thyme
¼ teaspoon
  lemon pepper
Salt to taste
12-ounce bag No Yolk
  extra broad noodles
2 cups chicken broth
2 tablespoons parsley

Combine the chicken broth, potatoes, tomatoes, onion, celery, cabbage and cauliflower in a large stockpot. Add the bay leaf, parsley, red pepper, pepper, sugar, garlic powder, oregano, basil, thyme, lemon pepper and salt. Simmer for 2 hours or until the vegetables are tender. Set aside. Prepare the noodles according to the package directions and drain. Pour 2 cups of the chicken broth over the noodles. Add the 2 tablespoons parsley and additional freshly-ground pepper. Serve the chowder over the noodles.

Serves 6

Tortellini Soup

6 pounds chicken breasts
1 gallon water
1 celery stalk
2 carrots, peeled and
    cut into 2-inch pieces
1 onion, quartered
3 parsley sprigs
8 black peppercorns
2 teaspoons salt
2 cups diced celery
½ cup shredded carrots
8 ounces sliced mushrooms

½ cup finely-
    chopped green onions
½ cup minced
    fresh parsley
1 bunch fresh spinach,
    shredded
2 boxes low-fat
    tomato-herb or garlic
    mozzarella tortellini
3 to 4 cups canned
    low-salt chicken broth
White pepper
    and salt to taste

Rinse the chicken and place it in a large stock pot. Add the water, celery, carrots, onion, parsley, peppercorns and salt. Bring the mixture to a boil, reduce the heat. Cover and simmer for 1 hour. Drain the chicken reserving the broth. Allow the chicken to cool and dice the meat. Cover and chill the chicken. Strain the broth again and chill overnight. Remove the layer of fat and discard. Pour the broth into a large stock pot and simmer. Add the chicken and the 2 cups of celery and 1/2 cup of shredded carrots. Add the mushrooms, green onions and minced parsley when the vegetables are almost tender. Add the spinach and cook for 10 minutes. Add the tortellini and chicken broth and cook for 15 minutes or until the tortellini is tender. Season with the white pepper and salt.

Serves 8

Carrots and Pineapple

1 bunch carrots
3 tablespoons butter

1 tablespoon sugar
8-ounce can
   crushed pineapple

Wash and peel the carrots. Cut the carrots into thin sticks about 3 inches long. Place the carrots in a saucepan and cover with salted water. Cook on a medium-low heat until the carrots are tender. Drain the carrots and return to the saucepan. Add the butter, sugar and pineapple. Heat until bubbly.

Serves 4

Cauliflower Stuffed Potatoes

This combination is an odd one, but you must try it to believe it's better than cheese alone!

4 to 6 baking potatoes
1 head cauliflower
2 cups nonfat milk

8 ounces light cheese
Salt and pepper to taste
Grated Parmesan cheese
Paprika

Bake the potatoes at 500 degrees for 45 minutes; do not wrap. Simmer the cauliflower in the milk in a saucepan for 12 to 15 minutes or until tender. Drain and set aside, reserving the milk. Scoop the inside of the baked potatoes, reserving the shells. Place the pulp in a large bowl and add the cauliflower, cheese, salt and pepper. Mash the potato mixture well with a potato masher. Add the reserved milk, a little at a time, to make a mixture the consistency of mashed potatoes. Fill the potato shells with the mixture. Sprinkle the potatoes with the Parmesan cheese and paprika.

Serves 4 to 6

Green Beans

2 pounds fresh green beans
3 chicken bouillon cubes
1 clove garlic, minced
½ teaspoon garlic salt
2 tablespoons dried minced onion
   or ½ cup fresh

1½ teaspoons sugar
1½ teaspoons salt
¼ to ½ teaspoon
   red pepper flakes
Parmesan cheese

We often put several small red potatoes on top of the beans during the last 25 minutes of cooking time.

Wash and break the green beans. Place the beans in a saucepan and barely cover with water. Add the bouillon, garlic, garlic salt, onion, sugar, salt and red pepper. Cover and cook over a medium heat for 1 to 1 ½ hours or until the beans are tender. Uncover and turn the heat to high and cook until nearly all of the water is gone. This helps the seasonings cook into the beans instead of staying in the water. Sprinkle with the Parmesan cheese and cover for 2 to 3 minutes or until the cheese has melted.

Serves 6

Hoppin' Johnny

This is a New Year's specialty or good on any nice cold winter day.

1-pound bag
   dry black-eyed peas
1 purple onion
1 green bell pepper
2 cloves garlic
6 to 8 ounces ham

2 teaspoons salt
¼ teaspoon pepper
10 drops of
   Tabasco sauce
4 cups cooked rice

Place the black-eyed peas in a large saucepan and cover with 3 inches of water. Bring the water to a boil and boil rapidly for 3 minutes. Remove from the heat and cover; allow to stand for 1 hour.

Finely chop the onion, bell pepper, garlic and ham. Add the salt, pepper and Tabasco sauce. Add the mixture to the peas. Cover and simmer for 3 hours. Remove the cover the last 30 minutes and turn the heat to medium-high. Allow the liquid to cook down until the peas look slightly thickened. The liquid should have the consistency of a thin gravy. Serve over of the rice.

Serves 8

Non-Fat Mashed Potatoes

Potatoes
Chicken bouillon cubes
Skim milk

Salt and white pepper
Fat free sour cream

Peel and quarter the potatoes. We use the yellow Yukon Gold butter tasting potatoes. Place the potatoes in a large saucepan and barely cover with water. Add 1 chicken bouillon cube for every three potatoes. Cook for 20 minutes or until the potatoes are tender. Drain and return the potatoes to the pan. Mash and add the skim milk for the right consistency. Season with the salt and white pepper. Stir in a dollop of the sour cream.

These potatoes are so good, no one will ever guess they are not made with butter and cream.

Steamed Artichokes

4 artichokes
6 tablespoons lemon juice
8 cloves garlic

4 teaspoons olive oil
6 teaspoons salt

Wash the artichokes. Cut off the stems. Trim the tops off by ¼ inch. Snap off the tough bottom leaves and trim the remaining leaves ¼ inch. Dip the artichokes in the lemon juice to prevent discoloration. Place the artichokes in a saucepan in 2 inches of boiling water. Add the garlic, lemon juice and salt. Steam, covered, for 45 minutes to 1 hour, depending on size. Drain the artichokes and serve with lemon wedges.

Pictured below, the artichoke is served with Basil Cream. However, we normally serve them plain to keep the fat content down. Many people like warm melted butter for dipping the leaves. If you are not worried about the fat, this is a delicious addition to the artichoke.

Printed in the USA
CPSIA information can be obtained
at www.ICGtesting.com
LVHW061924060124
768299LV00021B/45